Table of Co

I. Introduction
- 1. Outcomes & Indicators 3
- 2. Stories 7
- 3. Songs 10
- 4. Games & Activities 11
- 5. Crafts 22

II. Signs
- 1. Community 28
- 2. Fire & Police 37
- 3. Mail 46
- 4. Health Care 54
- 5. Construction 67
- 6. Occupation 73
- 7. Classroom 113
- 8. Days of the Week 153
- 9. Functional & Directional 161
- 10. Months 178
- 11. Time & Day 191

III. Common Classroom Phrases 211

IV. Handouts 226

V. Index 258

Copyright © 2008 Time to Sign, Inc.

Community and School

Outcomes & Indicators

The Child Outcomes and indicators are depicted as follows:
Domain
    Domain Element
        Indicators

A. Language Development

A.1 Listening & Understanding
- A.1.a. Sign language naturally demonstrates increased ability to understand and participate in conversations, stories, songs, rhythms, and games
- A.1.b. Sign language assists in the understanding and following of simple and multiple-step directions
- A.1.c. Sign language greatly increases children's receptive vocabulary
- A.1.d. Sign language assists non-English-speaking children in learning to listen to and understand English as well sign language

A.2 Speaking & Communication
- A.2.a. Sign language assists in developing increasing abilities to understand and use sign language and English to communicate information, experiences, ideas, feelings, opinions, needs, and questions for other purposes
- A.2.b. Sign language instruction teaches children the use of an increasingly complex and varied signed and spoken vocabulary
- A.2.c. Sign language assists non-English speaking children in signing and speaking English

B. Literacy

B.1 Phonological Awareness

As teachers say and sign words together it serves as another way for children to understand and remember both the sign and the spoken word. When taught together sign instruction assists in providing the following benefits.
- B.1.a. Progresses in recognizing matching sounds in familiar words, songs, rhythms, games, stories, and other activities
- B.1.b. Associates sounds with written and signed words
- B.1.c. Children's use of sign language enhances language acquisition
- B.1.d. Children's learning of sign language simultaneously with words assist in like word differentiation of emergent readers

B.2 Book Knowledge & Appreciation
- B.2.a. Signing is an enjoyable activity for children that greatly enhances vocabulary, which makes learning to read easier and sometimes earlier
- B.2.b. Children who are taught sign language demonstrate progress in abilities to retell, using sign words, stories from books and personal experiences

Copyright © 2008 Time to Sign, Inc.

- B.2.c. Children who are taught sign language demonstrate progress in abilities to act out stories in dramatic play which is a natural extension of the hand and finger movements learned in sign language

B.3 Print Awareness and Concepts
- B.3.a. Children who learn to sign develop a growing understanding of the different functions of forms of print such as signs, letters, and numbers
- B.3.b. When written words are presented with the verbal and sign introduction/instruction children better learn to recognize a word as a unit of print

B.4 Early Writing
- B.4.a. Begins to represent stories and experiences through signs, pictures, songs, games, and in play

B.5 Alphabet Knowledge
- B.5.a. Shows progress in associating the names of letters with their signs, shapes, and sounds
- B.5.b. Identifies all the letters of the alphabet, especially those in their own name
- B.5.c. Knows that the letters of the alphabet are a special category of visual graphics that can be individually signed and named

C. Mathematics

C.1 Number & Operations
- C.1.a. Children are taught the sign language counterparts to the numbers
- C.1.b. Children count numbers to assist with the retention of the number they have reached
- C.1.c. Signing assists with children's ability to count beyond the number 10
- C.1.d. Signing assists with children's learning to make use of one-to-one correspondence in counting objects and matching numbers of groups of objects

C.2 Geometry & Spatial Sense
- C.2.a. Signing assists with the recognition and ability to describe common shapes as shape signs accurately represent common shapes such as square, triangle, or circle
- C.2.b Signing assists children in developing visual and spatial awareness

D. Science

D.1 Scientific Skills & Methods
- D.1.a. Signing assists children in the understanding of scientific principles such as being able to express differences (such as big/little, open/closed, and more/less)
- D.1.b. Signing assists in increasing children's awareness
- D.1.c. Singing assists in the growing awareness of ideas and language related to time

Copyright © 2008 Time to Sign, Inc.

Community and School

D.2 Scientific Knowledge
- D.2.a. Signing assists in increasing awareness and beginning understanding of changes in material and cause-effect relationships
- D.2.b. Signing assists in increasing awareness of ideas and language related to time and temperature
- D.2.c. Signing assists in expanding knowledge of and respect for their body and the environment
- D.2.d. Signing enhances children's abilities to observe, describe and discuss the natural world, materials, living things, and natural processes

E. Creative Arts

E.1 Music

E.1.a. As children sign to music they develop increased interest and enjoyment in listening, singing, signing, finger plays, games, and performances

E.2 Movement

E.2.a. Children express through sign what is felt and heard in music

E.3 Dramatic Play

E.3.a. Children express themselves dramatically through signing

F. Social & Development

F.1 Self Concept

- F.1.a. Begins to develop and express awareness of self in terms of specific abilities, characteristics and preferences through the use of signing, for example they learn to sign their name and are given a sign name they feel reflects their personality
- F.1.b. Children's successful use of sign language enhances their confidence and self-esteem

F.2 Self Control

- F.2.a. Through the use of sign language children learn to express their feelings, emotions, needs, and opinions in everyday and in difficult situations without harming themselves, others, or property
- F.2.b. Through the use of sign language children demonstrate increased capacity to follows rules and routines, and to use materials purposefully, safely and respectfully
- F.2.c. Children's use of sign language raises communication awareness, enabling them to better tell and understand how their actions and words effect others
- F.2.d. Children's and teacher's use of sign language lowers children's noise levels in

the classroom enhancing the learning atmosphere
- F.2.e. Children's use of sign language teaches them to pay better attention, they need to pay attention visually, rather than just listen
- F.2.f. Children's use of sign language increase their use of manners, which can help to eliminate potential misbehavior reactions
- F.2.g Children's use of sign language fosters an atmosphere in which children ask questions before acting, for example asking if their classmate is done with the toy before taking it and angering their classmate
- F.2.h. Classroom usage of sign language engages the teachers to be present with the child, they need to be making regular eye contact and can better see in the faces of children if anything is wrong, the child is unhappy, etc.

F.3 Cooperation

- F.3.a. Children's use of sign language increases their abilities to sustain interactions with peers through the use of manners, enabling them to express their feelings and emotions, by helping, and by sharing
- F.3.b. Children's use of sign language increases their abilities to use compromise and discussion in playing and resolving conflicts with classmates
- F.3.c. Children's use of sign language increases their abilities to give and take in interactions; to take turns in games or using materials; and to be participatory in activities while not being overly aggressive

F.4 Social Relationships

- F.4.a. Children's use of sign language increases their signing and speaking with and accepting guidance and directions from a wide range of familiar adults
- F.4.b. Children and teacher's use of sign language in the classroom enables all in the classroom to develop friendships with peers, this is particularly true and key for any special needs members of the class.
- F.4.c. Children's use of sign language teaches them to be especially aware when classmates are in need, upset, hurt, or angry; and in expressing empathy for others

F.5 Knowledge of Families & Communities

- F.5.a. The Young Children's Signing Program incorporates family signs to assist in children's understanding of family composition
- F.5.b. The Young Children's Signing Program incorporates gender signs, boy and girl, to assist in children's understanding of genders

G. Approaches to Learning

G.1 Initiative & Curiosity

- G.1.a. Children's use of sign language increases participation in an increasing variety of tasks and activities
- G.1.b. Children's use of sign language enhances their use of imagination and inventiveness in participation in tasks and activities

Community and School

G.2 Engagement & Persistence
- G.2.a Children's learning of sign language also assist them as they increase their capacity to maintain concentration over time on a task, question, or set of directions or interactions

G.3 Reasoning & Problem Solving
- G.3.a. Children's learning and use of sign language assists in the recognition and problem solving through active exploration, including trial and error, and interactions and discussions with classmates and adults

H. Physical Health & Development

H.1. Fine Motor Skills
- H.1 a. Children's learning of sign language develops hand and arm strength and dexterity needed to control such instruments as a hammer, scissors, tape, and a stapler
- H.1.b. Children's learning of sign language develops hand-eye coordination required for use of building blocks, putting puzzles together, reproducing shapes and patterns, stringing beads, and using scissors
- H.1.c. Children's learning of sign language develops drawing and art tools such as pencils, crayons, markers, chalk, paint brushes, and computers
- H.1.d. Children's learning of sign language enables them to be able to pick up small objects

H.2 Gross Motor Skills
- H.2.a. Children's learning of sign language coordinates movements in throwing, catching, and bouncing balls

H.3 Health Status & Practices
- H.3.a. Children's learning of sign language enhances their ability to communicate health and hygiene problems to adults
- H.3.b. Children's learning of sign language enhances their knowledge of health and hygiene

Stories

<u>The Berenstain Bears Visit the Dentist</u> by Stan & Jan Berenstain (community)
Topical signs to be learned: sister, bear, brother, tooth (point to teeth), under, pillow, tell, mama, dentist, gentle, careful, look, water, seat, candy, balloon,.
Indicators: A.1.a, A.1.b, A.1.c, A.1.d, A.2.a, A.2.b, A.2.c, B.1.a, B.1.b, B.1.c, B.1.d, B.2.a, B.2.b, B.3.a, B.3.b, B.4.a, C.2.b, F.1.b, F.2.d, F.2.e, F.2.h, G.1.a, G.1.b, G.2.a, H.1.a, H.1.b, H.3.b.

<u>Community Helpers from A to Z</u> by Bobbie Kalman (community)
Topical signs to be learned: agricultural workers (farmer), business (busy), community,

Copyright © 2008 Time to Sign, Inc.

Community and School

help, doctor, dentist, firefighter, gymnastics coach (sign: jump several times for gymnastics), home helpers (help + agent), cook, clean, child care taker, car, airplane, journalist, kitchen staff (cook), server (waiter/waitress), librarian, mail carrier, nurse, police officer, house cleaner (clean + agent), plumber, mechanic, taxi driver (fingerspell t-a-x-i, sign drive + agent), teacher, vet, water, you, zoo keeper.
Indicators: A.1.a, A.1.b, A.1.c, A.1.d, A.2.a, A.2.b, A.2.c, B.1.a, B.1.b, B.1.c, B.1.d, B.2.a, B.3.a, B.4.a, C.2.b, F.1.b, F.2.d, F.2.e, F.2.h, G.1.a, G.1.b, G.2.a, H.1.a, H.1.b.

Cookie's Week by Cindy Ward & Tomie DePaola (School)
Topical signs to be learned: Monday, Tuesday, Wednesday, Thursday, Friday, Saturday, Sunday, Cookie, fell, toilet, knocked, plant, off, windowsill, dirt, everywhere, upset, trash, garbage, stuck, kitchen, drawer, pots, pans, dishes, ran, into, closet, before, door, closed, climbed, curtains, tomorrow, maybe, rest.
Indicators: A.1.a, A.1.b, A.1.c, A.1.d, A.2.a, A.2.b, A.2.c, B.1.a, B.1.b, B.1.c, B.1.d, B.2.a, B.2.b, B.3.a, B.3.b, B.4.a, C.2.b, F.1.b, F.2.d, F.2.e, F.2.h, G.1.a, G.1.b, G.2.a, H.1.a, H.1.b.

Fireman Small by Wong Herbert Lee (community)
Topical signs to be learned: town, little, man, fireman, small, firefighter, work, night, day, truck, nine, walk, bed, cat, tree, quick/fast, jump, pants, boots, ready, coat, fall, hooray, rabbit, safe, telephone, fire, hurry, thank you, help, good-bye.
Indicators: A.1.a, A.1.b, A.1.c, A.1.d, A.2.a, A.2.b, A.2.c, B.1.a, B.1.b, B.1.c, B.1.d, B.2.a, B.2.b, B.3.a, B.3.b, B.4.a, C.2.b, F.1.b, F.2.d, F.2.e, F.2.h, G.1.a, G.1.b, G.2.a, H.1.a, H.1.b.

Farm Flu by Teresa Bateman (community)
Topical signs to be learned: mom, farmer, farm, wet, dry, out, town, milk, cow, flu, sick, helped, bed, tissues, head, tea, pillows, dawn, chickens, soup, barnyard, chores, pig, turkeys, donkey, snacks, popcorn, relax, chess and checkers (games), sheep, little room, cleaned, rest (sleep), night, under, house, stop, listen, TV, toys, bed, miracle, magic, slow.
Indicators: A.1.a, A.1.b, A.1.c, A.1.d, A.2.a, A.2.b, A.2.c, B.1.a, B.1.b, B.1.c, B.1.d, B.2.a, B.2.b, B.3.a, B.3.b, B.4.a, C.2.b, F.1.b, F.2.d, F.2.e, F.2.h, G.1.a, G.1.b, G.2.a, H.1.a, H.1.b.

Five Little Monkeys by Eileen Christelow (available in Spanish)
Topical signs to be learned: five, little, monkeys, jumping, on, bed, fell, off, bumped, head, Mama, called, Doctor, said, No more, four, three, two, one, zero.
Indicators: A.1.a, A.1.b, A.1.c, A.1.d, A.2.a, A.2.b, A.2.c, B.1.a, B.1.b, B.1.c, B.1.d, B.2.a, B.2.b, B.3.a, B.3.b, B.4.a, C.1.a, C.1.b, C.1.d, C.2.b, F.1.b, F.2.d, F.2.e, F.2.h, F.4.a, G.1.a, G.1.b, G.2.a, H.1.a, H.1.b.

Family and Community by Jane Schneider and Kathy Kifer (community)
Topical signs to be learned: family, neighborhood, emergency workers, school, sports, stores, on the town, construction, news and legal, and other occupations.
Indicators: A.1.a, A.1.b, A.1.c, A.1.d, A.2.a, A.2.b, A.2.c, B.1.a, B.1.b, B.1.c, B.1.d, B.2.a, B.2.b, B.3.a, B.3.b, B.4.a, C.2.b, F.1.b, F.2.d, F.2.e, F.2.h, F.4.a, G.1.a, G.1.b, G.2.a, H.1.a, H.1.b

A Letter to Amy by Ezra Jack Keats (mail, friends)
Topical signs to be learned: write, letter, invite (welcome), party, ask, mother, special, envelope, mail (send), please, come, birthday, Saturday, stamp, rain, coat, mailbox, sky, dark, cloud, boy, see, girl, lightening, thunder, wind, chase, can't, catch, look for, run, cry,

Copyright © 2008 Time to Sign, Inc.

Community and School

birthday, cake, wait, now, candle.
Indicators: A.1.a, A.1.b, A.1.c, A.1.d, A.2.a, A.2.b, A.2.c, B.1.a, B.1.b, B.1.c, B.1.d, B.2.a, B.2.b, B.3.a, B.4.a, B.3.b, C.2.b, F.1.b, F.2.d, F.2.e, F.2.h, F.5.a, G.1.a, G.1.b, G.2.a, H.1.a, H.1.b

Library Lil by Suzanne Williams (community)
Topical signs to be learned: library, librarian, old, lady, shh/quiet, always, kid, imagine, read, fast, strong, carry, book, surprise, story (also: tell story), new, tv, evil/bad, storm, dark, push, every, person, week, motorcycle, laugh, who, where, move, open, fight.
Indicators: A.1.a, A.1.b, A.1.c, A.1.d, A.2.a, A.2.b, A.2.c, B.1.a, B.1.b, B.1.c, B.1.d, B.2.a, B.2.b, B.3.a, B.3.b, B.4.a, C.2.b, F.1.b, F.2.d, F.2.e, F.2.h, G.1.a, G.1.b, G.2.a, H.1.a, H.1.b

Market Day by Lois Ehlert (community (available in Spanish)
Topical signs to be learned: red, morning, chicken, corn, carrots, dirt, tomato, shirt, turkey, gate, escape?, truck, ready, go, pass, fields, vegetables, grow, bird, tree, snake, fish, frog, bridge, sheep, all, market/store?, town, buy/sell, work, play, day, road, wheels, home, eat.
Indicators: A.1.a, A.1.b, A.1.c, A.1.d, A.2.a, A.2.b, A.2.c, B.1.a, B.1.b, B.1.c, B.1.d, B.2.a, B.2.b, B.3.a, B.3.b, B.4.a, C.2.b, F.1.b, F.2.d, F.2.e, F.2.h, G.1.a, G.1.b, G.2.a, H.1.a, H.1.b

Miss Nelson Is Missing! By Harry Allard (available in Spanish)
Topical signs to be learned: room, class, all, school, calm down, not, laugh, story, terrible, ugly, new, teacher, math, book, still, work, miss, find, police, house, hello, children, silly, sing, never, tell.
Indicators: A.1.a, A.1.b, A.1.c, A.1.d, A.2.a, A.2.b, A.2.c, B.1.a, B.1.b, B.1.c, B.1.d, B.2.a, B.2.b, B.3.a, B.4.a, B.3.b, C.2.b, F.1.b, F.2.d, F.2.e, F.2.h, G.1.a, G.1.b, G.2.a, H.1.a, H.1.b.

Office Buckle and Gloria by Peggy Rathmann (community)
Topical signs to be learned: office, police, safety, never, school, listen, dog, sit, shoe, look, always, clean up, fall, good, laugh, surprise, funny, thank you, letter, student, picture, star, telephone, please, bring, ice cream, friend, swimming, storm, good morning, sleep, kiss, best, stay, with, your.
Indicators: A.1.a, A.1.b, A.1.c, A.1.d, A.2.a, A.2.b, A.2.c, B.1.a, B.1.b, B.1.c, B.1.d, B.2.a, B.2.b, B.3.a, B.4.a, B.3.b, C.2.b, F.1.b, F.2.d, F.2.e, F.2.h, G.1.a, G.1.b, G.2.a, H.1.a, H.1.b.

Please Play Safe: Penguin's Guide to Playground Safety by Margery Cuyler
Topical signs to be learned: friend, go, playground, run, fast, right, wrong, no, walk, not, hurt, play, jump, off, wait, want, slide, climb, turn, catch, throw, ball, ready, sand, box, face, ask, help, dig, see, gentle, back, swing, stop, leave, bring.
Indicators: A.1.a, A.1.b, A.1.c, A.1.d, A.2.a, A.2.b, A.2.c, B.1.a, B.1.b, B.1.c, B.1.d, B.2.a, B.2.b, B.3.a, B.3.b, B.4.a, F.1.b, F.2.b, F.2.c, F.2.d, F.2.e, F.2.h, F.4.a, F.4.b, F.4.c, G.1.a, G.1.b, G.2.a, H.1.a, H.1.b.

Today is Monday by Eric Carle
Topical signs to be learned: today, Monday, Tuesday, spaghetti, Wednesday, Thursday, meat, Friday, fish, Saturday, chicken, Sunday, ice cream, hungry, children, come, eat, snake, elephant, cat, bird, monkey.
Indicators: A.1.a, A.1.b, A.1.c, A.1.d, A.2.a, A.2.b, A.2.c, B.1.a, B.1.b, B.1.c, B.1.d, B.2.a, B.2.b, B.3.a, B.3.b, B.4.a, C.2.b, D.1.c, D.2.b, F.1.b, F.2.d, F.2.e, F.2.h, G.1.a, G.1.b, G.2.a, H.1.a, H.1.b.

Copyright © 2008 Time to Sign, Inc.

<u>Walter the Baker</u> by Eric Carle (community)
Topical signs to be learned: baker, town, wife, son, best, bred, cake, cookies, store, sell, eat, morning, cat, milk, water, mad, leave, home, please, sun, good, work, all, day, night, make, shape signs, clean, throw, salt, look, basket, pretzel, afternoon, glad/happy.
Indicators: A.1.a, A.1.b, A.1.c, A.1.d, A.2.a, A.2.b, A.2.c, B.1.a, B.1.b, B.1.c, B.1.d, B.2.a, B.2.b, B.3.a, B.3.b, B.4.a, C.2.b, F.1.b, F.2.d, F.2.e, F.2.h, G.1.a, G.1.b, G.2.a, G.3.a, H.1.a, H.1.b.

<u>Will I Have a Friend?</u> By Miriam Cohen
Topical signs to be learned: pa, school, friend, good-bye, come, teacher, boy, girl, where, blocks, table, cold, wet, heavy, orange juice, cookie, finished, laugh, story time, sit, read, book, monkey, rest, play, home.
Indicators: A.1.a, A.1.b, A.1.c, A.1.d, A.2.a, A.2.b, A.2.c, B.1.a, B.1.b, B.1.c, B.1.d, B.2.a, B.2.b, B.3.a, B.3.b, B.4.a, C.2.b, F.1.b, F.2.d, F.2.e, F.2.h, F.4.b, G.1.a, G.1.b, G.2.a H.1.a, H.1.b.

Songs

I'm a Firefighter (community)
Indicators: A.1.a, A.1.b, A.1.c, A.1.d, A.2.a, A.2.b, A.2.c, B.1.a, B.1.c, B.1.d, B.2.a, B.2.b, B.3.a, B.4.a, C.2.b, E.1.a, E.2.a, F.1.b, F.2.e, F.2.h, F.3.c, G.1.a, G.1.b, H.1.a, H.1.b, H.1.d

I'm a Little Police Officer (community)
Indicators: A.1.a, A.1.b, A.1.c, A.1.d, A.2.a, A.2.b, A.2.c, B.1.a, B.1.c, B.1.d, B.2.a, B.2.b, B.3.a, B.4.a, C.2.b, E.1.a, E.2.a, F.1.b, F.2.e, F.2.h, F.3.c, G.1.a, G.1.b, H.1.a, H.1.b, H.1.d

I've Been Working on the Railroad – (occupations)
Indicators: A.1.a, A.1.b, A.1.c, A.1.d, A.2.a, A.2.b, A.2.c, B.1.a, B.1.c, B.1.d, B.2.a, B.2.b, B.3.a, B.4.a, C.2.b, E.1.a, E.2.a, F.1.b, F.2.e, F.2.h, F.3.c, G.1.a, G.1.b, H.1.a, H.1.b, H.1.d

Make New Friends – (friends)
Indicators: A.1.a, A.1.b, A.1.c, A.1.d, A.2.a, A.2.b, A.2.c, B.1.a, B.1.c, B.1.d, B.2.a, B.2.b, B.3.a, B.4.a, C.2.b, E.1.a, E.2.a, F.1.b, F.2.e, F.2.h, F.3.c, F.4.b, G.1.a, G.1.b, H.1.a, H.1.b, H.1.d

March and Sing (functional/directional)
Indicators: A.1.a, A.1.b, A.1.c, A.1.d, A.2.a, A.2.b, A.2.c, B.1.a, B.1.c, B.1.d, B.2.a, B.2.b, B.3.a, B.4.a, C.2.b, E.1.a, E.2.a, F.1.b, F.2.e, F.2.h, F.3.c, G.1.a, G.1.b, H.1.a, H.1.b, H.1.d

More We Sign Together, The (friends)
Indicators: A.1.a, A.1.b, A.1.c, A.1.d, A.2.a, A.2.b, A.2.c, B.1.a, B.1.c, B.1.d, B.2.a, B.2.b, B.3.a, B.4.a, C.2.b, E.1.a, E.2.a, F.1.b, F.2.e, F.2.h, F.3.c, F.4.b, G.1.a, G.1.b, H.1.a, H.1.b, H.1.d

My Dentist (health)
Indicators: A.1.a, A.1.b, A.1.c, A.1.d, A.2.a, A.2.b, A.2.c, B.1.a, B.1.c, B.1.d, B.2.a, B.2.b, B.3.a, B.4.a, C.2.b, E.1.a, E.2.a, F.1.b, F.2.e, F.2.h, F.3.c, G.1.a, G.1.b, H.1.a, H.1.b, H.1.d, H.3.a, H.3.b

Community and School

The School Bus Comes for Me (school)
Indicators: A.1.a, A.1.b, A.1.c, A.1.d, A.2.a, A.2.b, A.2.c, B.1.a, B.1.c, B.1.d, B.2.a, B.2.b, B.3.a, B.4.a, C.2.b, E.1.a, E.2.a, F.1.b, F.2.e, F.2.h, F.3.c, G.1.a, G.1.b, H.1.a, H.1.b, H.1.d

We've Been Playing (school)
Indicators: A.1.a, A.1.b, A.1.c, A.1.d, A.2.a, A.2.b, A.2.c, B.1.a, B.1.c, B.1.d, B.2.a, B.2.b, B.3.a, B.4.a, C.2.b, E.1.a, E.2.a, F.1.b, F.2.e, F.2.h, F.3.c, F.4.b, G.1.a, G.1.b, H.1.a, H.1.b, H.1.d

What's My Job – (occupations)
Indicators: A.1.a, A.1.b, A.1.c, A.1.d, A.2.a, A.2.b, A.2.c, B.1.a, B.1.c, B.1.d, B.2.a, B.2.b, B.3.a, B.4.a, C.2.b, E.1.a, E.2.a, F.1.b, F.2.e, F.2.h, F.3.c, G.1.a, G.1.b, H.1.a, H.1.b, H.1.d

Wheels on the Bus (school)
Indicators: A.1.a, A.1.b, A.1.c, A.1.d, A.2.a, A.2.b, A.2.c, B.1.a, B.1.c, B.1.d, B.2.a, B.2.b, B.3.a, B.4.a, C.2.b, E.1.a, E.2.a, F.1.b, F.2.e, F.2.h, F.3.c, G.1.a, G.1.b, H.1.a, H.1.b, H.1.d

Who Came to School Today? (school and names)
Indicators: A.1.a, A.1.b, A.1.c, A.1.d, A.2.a, A.2.b, A.2.c, B.1.a, B.1.c, B.1.d, B.2.a, B.2.b, B.3.a, B.4.a, C.2.b, E.1.a, E.2.a, F.1.b, F.2.e, F.2.h, F.3.c, F.4.b, G.1.a, G.1.b, H.1.a, H.1.b, H.1.d

Games & Activities

Bus Scene (transportation)
Materials: large sheet of butcher or craft paper to make a bus mural, markers, crayons, or pencils, tape, stapler or pushpins, scissors; bus props such as baby car seat, chairs, blocks or boxes to sit on, dolls or toys as passengers, newspaper, magazines, books, plastic jar for collecting fares, poker chips for play money, real steering wheels, shopping bag, backpack, package.

Design the bus wall scenery on a large piece of butcher paper but in a bus shape (don't forget wheels). Draw big rectangles to indicate windows. In each window, draw or paste a picture of a scene that someone might see if looking out the bus windows (real life or completely imaginary or fantasy). Attach the bus mural to the wall with the wheels just touching the floor, just beside the bus, set up the seats (At least four but no more than ten). Now play bus! The driver collects fares, passengers come and go whenever they reach their stops. Everyone sings "The Wheels on the Bus"!
You can play taxi, train, airplane, or other mode of transportation. You can add dress-up clothes to the pretend scene of the people riding the transportation.

Topical signs to be learned: bus, wheels, drive, wipers, draw, window, door, seat/chair, money, pay, people, come, go, sit, book, bag, backpack.
Indicators: A.1.a, A.1.b, A.1.c, A.1.d, A.2.a, A.2.b, A.2.c, B.1.c, B.2.a, B.2.b, B.2.c, C.2.b, E.3.a, F.1.b, F.2.a, F.2.b, F.2.c, F.2.d, F.2.e, F.2.f, F.2.g, F.2.h, F.3.a, F.3.b, F.3.c, F.4.b, F.4.c, G.1.a, G.1.b, G.2.a, G.3.a, H.1.a, H.1.b, H.1.d, H.2.a.

Copyright © 2008 Time to Sign, Inc.

Calendar Counting (school, months, days of the week)
Materials: calendar.

This can be an activity done everyday such as during circle time. Be sure to have the calendar in a convenient place where children can see and reach it. In the beginning focus on the days of the week such as how many days are in a week, what the names of the days of the week are, how many days have passed so far and how many days are left. Mark out each day as it passes. Also talk about the months of the year and the numbers in a month. You can count how many days have passed so far in the month, how many are left, etc.

Topical signs to be learned: yesterday, tomorrow, today, numbers 1-31, days of the week, months of the year, year, month, what, when, how many.
Indicators: A.1.a, A.1.b, A.1.c, A.1.d, A.2.a, A.2.b, A.2.c, B.1.c, B.2.a, B.2.b, B.2.c, C.1.a, C.1.b, C.1.c, C.1.d, C.2.b, D.1.c, D.1.c, F.1.b, F.2.b, F.2.d, F.2.e, F.2.h, F.3.a, F.3.c, F.4.b, G.1.a, G.1.b, G.2.a, G.3.a, H.1.b, H.1.d.

Classroom Helper Chart (school)
How will your helpers be chosen? What tasks would you like to select for the children to do? Things like lead the flag salute, take the attendance and lunch count folders to the office, help pass out papers, etc. Make your own classroom helper chart and get a system down before the first day of school. Children feel a sense of pride fulfilling daily tasks and you save yourself some time.

Topical signs to be learned: helper (help + agent), choose, do, line leader (line-up + lead + agent), clean-up....
Indicators: A.1.a, A.1.b, A.1.c, A.1.d, A.2.a, A.2.b, A.2.c, B.1.c, B.2.a, B.2.b, B.2.c, C.2.b, F.1.a, F.1.b, F.2.b, F.2.c, F.2.d, F.2.e, F.2.h, F.3.a, F.4.a, F.4.b, G.1.a, G.1.b, G.2.a, G.3.a, H.1.b, H.1.d.

Dentist (community, occupations)
Discuss the importance of taking good care of our teeth, including demonstrating how to brush, eating the right foods and visiting the Dentist.

Topical signs to be learned: teeth, mouth, tooth, toothbrush, Dentist.
Indicators: A.1.a, A.1.b, A.1.c, A.1.d, A.2.a, A.2.b, A.2.c, B.1.c, B.2.a, B.2.b, B.2.c, C.2.b, F.1.b, F.2.b, F.2.c, F.2.d, F.2.e, F.2.h, F.3.a, F.3.b, F.3.c, F.4.b, G.1.a, G.1.b, G.2.a, G.3.a, H.1.a, H.1.b, H.1.d, H.3.a, H.3.b.

Dramatic Play: Astronaut (occupations)
Materials: appliance box cut apart to stand like scenery, anything covered with aluminum foil (blocks, kitchen utensils, toys), paper grocery bag helmets (cut to just past the ears), jump suits or clothing that looks like jump suits, boots, goggles, gloves, pictures of planets and outer space (optional), art material for making helmets, control panel, space suits, crayons, markers, glue, tape, stapler, hole punch, scissors, control panel for rocket ships made with a few of the following materials: aluminum foil, bottle caps, bubble wrap, large sheet of cardboard for panel, milk jug lids, old head sets, old microphone, orange juice caps, telephone cords, curly spirals, cereal box, hose scraps, milk jug, potato chip or oatmeal box, paper towel tubes, colorful scrap telephone wire or scrap cable, andf computer monitor.

Community and School

To play Astronaut, cut apart an appliance box and stand it up to make a small room that will be the rocket ship. Use art supplies to build a control panel with lots of buttons, knobs, dials, screens, and wires. Glue, tape, and staple them to a sheet of cardboard on the table. Wrap anything in aluminum foil, including the astronauts' arms and legs, to enhance space play. Make helmets and space suits from material on hand (Milk jugs can be helmets, boxes can be air tanks or jet packs, paper towel tubes can be a telescope, etc.) Tack pictures of outer space and other planets to the walls and around the control panel (optional). Now blast off for outer space!

Topical signs to be learned: astronaut, rocket, moon, stars, sun, boots, glue, box, computer, numbers 1-10.
Indicators: A.1.a, A.1.b, A.1.c, A.1.d, A.2.a, A.2.b, A.2.c, B.1.c, B.2.a, B.2.b, B.2.c, C.2.b, E.3.a, F.1.b, F.2.a, F.2.b, F.2.c, F.2.d, F.2.e, F.2.f, F.2.g, F.3.a, F.3.b, F.3.c, F.4.b, F.4.c, G.1.a, G.1.b, G.2.a, G.3.a, H.1.a, H.1.b, H.1.d, H.2.a.

Dramatic Play: Bank (occupations)
Materials: table and chairs or boxes, large quantity of play money (Photocopy real money and cut out, use play money from games, or draw money on slips of paper. Bingo markers, poker chips, and buttons make good coins), cardboard or real computer, pencils, pens, scrap paper, telephones, crayons, markers, glue, tape, scissors, adding machines or calculators, cash box with money tray, checkbooks, gold bricks (painted blocks of wood), money bags, pencil tired to yarn and taped to table, play credit cards and card machine, safe (cardboard box with lock drawn on it), safety deposit boxes (shoeboxes with numbers written on them), savings books.

Set up a play corner centered around the teller's table and a desk and chair. Some of the bank people would be teller, bank president, loan representative, and customer. Take turns playing different parts. Bank play will depend on experience. It may be as simple as depositing money or writing a check. Some of the on-going business at a bank includes depositing money, withdrawing money, writing checks, putting valuables in a safety deposit box, taking out a loan for a car, financing a home.

Topical signs to be learned: bank, banker, president, table, chair, money, count, change, computer, pencil, pen, telephone, call, bag, savings (save), money signs, number signs.
Indicators: A.1.a, A.1.b, A.1.c, A.1.d, A.2.a, A.2.b, A.2.c, B.1.c, B.2.a, B.2.b, B.2.c, C.2.b, E.3.a, F.1.b, F.2.a, F.2.b, F.2.c, F.2.d, F.2.e, F.2.f, F.2.g, F.3.a, F.3.b, F.3.c, F.4.b, F.4.c, G.1.a, G.1.b, G.2.a, G.3.a, H.1.a, H.1.b, H.1.d, H.2.a.

Dramatic Play: Carpenter (occupations)
Materials: sturdy work table, wood scraps (all shapes and sizes), sandpaper, hammers, saws, screwdrivers and other tools; nails and screws (many different types), goggles, wood glue, carpenter's apron or tool belt, carpenter's pencil, colored masking tape, filter masks, gold paint and brush (optional), ruler, tape measure, tool box, wood putty, wood screws, working hand drill.

Find a sturdy work table at child height that is able to take some hammering and nailing, sanding and painting. Arrange the supplies in boxes or on a shelf near the work table.

Copyright © 2008 Time to Sign, Inc.

Stack wood scraps underneath the table in boxes. Begin woodworking. Some of the activities that might occur are drilling holes for screws, hammering and nailing, measuring, painting, sanding, and screwing in wood screws. Make real things, or simply work with wood. Make sure to have adult supervision when students are using tools.

Topical sings to be learned: carpenter, tools, glue, pencil, tool box, work, table, build, measure, paint.
Indicators: A.1.a, A.1.b, A.1.c, A.1.d, A.2.a, A.2.b, A.2.c, B.1.c, B.2.a, B.2.b, B.2.c, C.2.b, E.3.a, F.1.b, F.2.a, F.2.b, F.2.c, F.2.d, F.2.e, F.2.f, F.2.g, F.3.a, F.3.b, F.3.c, F.4.b, F.4.c, G.1.a, G.1.b, G.2.a, G.3.a, H.1.a, H.1.b, H.1.d, H.2.a.

Dramatic Play: Florist (occupations)

Materials: work table, soil in water table or plastic trays, pots, cups, vases, baskets, milk cartons and containers of all kinds; live or plastic flowers and plants, ribbons, raffia, small cards or old greeting cards with flowers, stickers (for prices), art supplies such as crayons, markers, scissors, glue, tape, stapler, paper; telephone, books about flowers, brochures for florists, play cash register (or one made from a cardboard box), gardening gloves, note pad and pencil for orders, pictures of flowers, play money, shallow cardboard boxes for transporting pots or displaying plants, smocks or aprons, tissue or newsprint to wrap flowers, watering can.

Set up a work table for arranging flowers as well as planting and caring for them. Things to do in the florist shop could include: taking orders on the phone, arranging flowers in pots with soil or vases with water, Arrange flowers in pots with soil, or in vases with water (if possible, use live plants and flowers), decorating greeting cards, selling flowers and arrangements to customers, etc. Take arrangements apart and play florist all over again. You can make flowers out of cupcakes liners glued on sticks, dyed coffee filters on pipe cleaners, paper for blossoms and wire for stems. Or make dried or pressed flowers.

Topical signs to be learned: flowers, florist, store, plant, care, store, soil/dirt, water, decorate, ribbon, crayon, scissors, glue, paper, telephone, book, gloves, garden, table.
Indicators: A.1.a, A.1.b, A.1.c, A.1.d, A.2.a, A.2.b, A.2.c, B.1.c, B.2.a, B.2.b, B.2.c, C.2.b, E.3.a, F.1.b, F.2.a, F.2.b, F.2.c, F.2.d, F.2.e, F.2.f, F.2.g, F.3.a, F.3.b, F.3.c, F.4.b, F.4.c, G.1.a, G.1.b, G.2.a, G.3.a, H.1.a, H.1.b, H.1.d, H.2.a.

Dramatic Play: Office (occupations)

Materials: pens, pencils, tape, stapler, paper, envelopes, stickers for stamps, telephones (two is better than one), desk and chairs (or boxes), clip board, scissors, hole punch, old typewriter, coffee cups, coffee pot, adding machine or calculator, photograph of family member for desk (optional), clock (old clock for play, or make one from cardboard with moveable hands), boxes to make into computers, copy machine, cubby holes/mail slots, file drawer, scanner, trash can (draw knobs and buttons on them to resemble the machines).

Set up a desk or table as the central prop, and organize the rest of the office around it. Arrange envelopes, stamps, and paper for letter writing. Prepare the desk with a few office props. If desired, have refreshments like coffee and tea on hand. Spend time working very hard in the office. When the day is over, it's time to go home from work.

Community and School

Topical signs to be learned: secretary, work, pen, pencil, paper, envelope, stamp, write, scissors, desk, chair, computer, cubby, telephone, coffee, tea, cup, day, over (finished), go, home.
Indicators: A.1.a, A.1.b, A.1.c, A.1.d, A.2.a, A.2.b, A.2.c, B.1.c, B.2.a, B.2.b, B.2.c, C.2.b, E.3.a, F.1.b, F.2.a, F.2.b, F.2.c, F.2.d, F.2.e, F.2.f, F.2.g, F.3.a, F.3.b, F.3.c, F.4.b, F.4.c, G.1.a, G.1.b, G.2.a, G.3.a, H.1.a, H.1.b, H.1.d, H.2.a.

Dramatic Play: School

Materials: chalkboard and chalk, dry erase board and markers, or square of cardboard and chalk; paper, crayons, pencils, pens, erasers, chalkboard eraser; desks, tables, chairs, or boxes; favorite dolls or toys as students, bell, books, clock, colored stick-on stars, flag, learning games, music/tapes for signing time, stickers.

Set up a school area with a chalkboard, dry erase board, or square of cardboard as the center of learning. (Chalk will wipe off the cardboard nicely. Dry erase boards work well with markers. Use an old sock for the eraser.) Place boxes or chairs around the board, or set up desks or boxes for desks. Everyone sits at a table or desk, and take turns being the teacher. If stuffed toys are attending school, encourage them to try hard and they will get a sticker for work well done! Play school in all its wide variety of activities, like art, gym, lunch or snack, nap time, recess, singing, dancing, walk to school or ride in a play bus or car, writing and reading.

Topical signs to be learned: school, blackboard, chalk, pen, pencil, paper, desk, table, chair, teacher, student, learn, teach, art, recess, band, write, read, study, bus, ride, lunch, snack.
Indicators: A.1.a, A.1.b, A.1.c, A.1.d, A.2.a, A.2.b, A.2.c, B.1.c, B.2.a, B.2.b, B.2.c, C.2.b, E.3.a, F.1.b, F.2.a, F.2.b, F.2.c, F.2.d, F.2.e, F.2.f, F.2.g, F.3.a, F.3.b, F.3.c, F.4.b, F.4.c, G.1.a, G.1.b, G.2.a, G.3.a, H.1.a, H.1.b, H.1.d, H.2.a.

Dramatic Play: Veterinarian (occupations, animals)

Materials: stuffed toy animals, medical tools and supplies (real or handmade) such as: ace bandage, Band-Aids, cotton balls, empty lotion bottle, empty pill bottle, stethoscope, surgical gown and cap, tape (masking tape), thermometer, tongue depressors, toy doctor kit supplies; table, telephone, weighing scale, animal treats, animal x-rays (donated by local vet office) or children can draw x-rays, cardboard boxes for animal carry cases and kennels, clipboard, notebook and pencil, pretend x-ray machine (made from cardboard box).

Playing vet is very much like playing doctor, except the focus is on a pet, not a person. This is precisely why children love to explore the medical aspects of examining and treating a toy pet—they are often basing their experiences on themselves and their own visits to the pediatrician. Set up a vets office centered around the examining table. Have toy pets visit the vet for examination and treatment. Some of the situations that often evolve in play are broken bones, cuts or bruises, diseases, hurt head, ear, eye, leg, foot, paw, tummy; loneliness, needs a family (lives at the pound, is lost, is abandoned). Often prescriptions or appointments are needed, including telephone calls and detailed consultations and treatments. Return visits are common.

Topical signs to be learned: pet and animal signs, veterinarian, hurt, pain, head, nurse, doctor, sick, heart, head, treat, medicine, better, feel, earache, healthy (health).

Copyright © 2008 Time to Sign, Inc.

Indicators: A.1.a, A.1.b, A.1.c, A.1.d, A.2.a, A.2.b, A.2.c, B.1.c, B.2.a, B.2.b, B.2.c, C.2.b, E.3.a, F.1.b, F.2.a, F.2.b, F.2.c, F.2.d, F.2.e, F.2.f, F.2.g, F.3.a, F.3.b, F.3.c, F.4.b, F.4.c, G.1.a, G.1.b, G.2.a, G.3.a, H.1.a, H.1.b, H.1.d, H.2.a.

Energy Community Helpers (community, occupations)

Materials: magazines and catalogs, scissors, poster board, glue, clear adhesive paper, markers.

Cut out pictures of workers using different types of energy (firefighter, electrician, phone line worker, TV repairperson, jackhammer operator, computer operator, construction worker etc.) Glue the pictures on poster board, and cover them with clear adhesive paper.

Show the pictures of the community helpers. Have the children identify what each person does. Talk about the types of energy the people use or deal with in their work. Discuss the importance of the work these people do for us. Or you can have the children find pictures themselves and explain to the group what their worker does and the type of energy they use in their work.

Topical signs to be learned: community, help, magazine, scissors, glue, occupation signs, picture, work.
Indicators: A.1.a, A.1.b, A.1.c, A.1.d, A.2.a, A.2.b, A.2.c, B.1.c, B.2.a, B.2.b, B.2.c, C.2.b, F.1.b, F.2.b, F.2.c, F.2.d, F.2.e, F.2.h, F.3.a, F.3.b, F.3.c, G.1.a, G.1.b, G.2.a, G.3.a, H.1.b, H.1.d

Fast, Friendly Firefighters (fire & police)

Talk about how a firefighter puts out a fire. Then have the children act out going to a fire and putting it out from the bell ringing in the firehouse to the fire being put out and the firefighters going back to the firehouse.

Topical signs to be learned: firefighter, fire, smoke, fast, friendly, help, fire truck, sleep, bell, water, rescue (save/safe).
Indicators: A.1.a, A.1.b, A.1.c, A.1.d, A.2.a, A.2.b, A.2.c, B.1.c, B.2.a, B.2.b, B.2.c, C.2.b, E.3.a, F.1.b, F.2.b, F.2.c, F.2.d, F.2.e, F.2.h, F.3.a, F.3.c, F.4.a, G.1.a, G.1.b, G.2.a, H.1.d, H.2.a.

Fire Drill (fire & police)

Even though you are expected to do fire drills on a regular basis, have your class do a fire drill during the theme.

Topical signs to be learned: fire, line up, 9-1-1-, telephone, stay calm, outside, safety.
Indicators: A.1.a, A.1.b, A.1.c, A.1.d, A.2.a, A.2.b, A.2.c, B.1.c, B.2.a, B.2.b, B.2.c, C.2.b, F.1.b, F.2.b, F.2.c, F.2.d, F.2.e, F.2.h, F.4.a, G.1.a, G.2.a, H.1.d, H.2.a.

Fire Engine (fire & police)

This game can have 5-50+ players. First, divide the group into lines of five or six players. Have them all make parallel lines pointing in the same direction. We pretend that there is about 50 feet in front of the line, and we send the first person (or fire engine) in each line with their siren wailing (their vocalization) and light flashing (an arm flailing over the

Community and School

head) to put the fire out. When the engine/person gets to the fire, they become a fire person holding a fire hose shooting water on the fire. But it turns out to be a big fire, so the first engine goes back to the line to get a second engine/person, wailing and flailing the whole time. They both race off holding hands to put out the fire. This repeats until every person in each line has been fetched.

Topical signs to be learned: fire engine, line, light, fire, water, fire, big.
Indicators: A.1.a, A.1.b, A.1.c, A.1.d, A.2.a, A.2.b, A.2.c, B.1.c, B.2.a, B.2.b, B.2.c, C.2.b, F.1.b, F.2.b, F.2.c, F.2.d, F.2.e, F.2.h, F.3.c, G.1.a, G.2.a, H.1.d, H.2.a.

Fire Extinguisher Tag (fire & police)
Have some children pretend to be blazing, hot fires and have other children pretend to be fire extinguishers. The fire extinguishers sit down as the other children pantomime the beginning of a fire: The fire is just beginning to burn (The children squat down close to the floor.) The flames are getting bigger. (The children kneel.) The wind is picking up. (The children sway back and forth on knees.) Now the fire is blazing hot. (The children jump up and down.) The fire is spreading. (The children run around.) Here come the fire extinguishers! (The fire extinguishers catch and tag the fire children.) When a fire child has been tagged, the fire extinguisher says "Zzzzzzza," and the fire child is extinguished and lies down. After all fire children are lying down, the fire extinguishers can also rest.

Topical signs to be learned: hot, fire, pretend, sit, wind, touch, lie down.
Indicators: A.1.a, A.1.b, A.1.c, A.1.d, A.2.a, A.2.b, A.2.c, B.1.c, B.2.a, B.2.b, B.2.c, C.2.b, F.1.b, F.2.b, F.2.c, F.2.d, F.2.e, F.2.h, F.3.c, G.1.a, G.2.a, H.1.d, H.2.a.

Firefighter Visit (fire & police)
Invite a firefighter to come and talk with your children. Most fire departments already have a program set up for this. They may bring a fire truck and talk about fire safety.

Topical signs to be learned: firefighter, fire truck, fire, safety, don't be afraid.
Indicators: A.1.a, A.1.b, A.1.c, A.1.d, A.2.a, A.2.b, A.2.c, B.1.c, B.2.a, B.2.b, B.2.c, C.2.b, F.1.b, F.2.b, F.2.c, F.2.d, F.2.e, F.2.h, F.4.a, G.1.a, G.2.a, H.1.d, H.2.a.

Fire Prevention Week (fire & police)
This is the first week in October. It's important for children to be aware of the benefits and dangers of fire.

Elicit suggestions from the children for helping to prevent fires. (Don't leave oily dust cloths in a closet. Never play with a lighter, matches, or a gas stove. Make sure a grownup's burning cigarette is not left on the edge of a counter or table.) Talk with the children about what to do if there's a fire in school. How should we act? (Keep calm. Walk quickly out the nearest door. Why should we all walk and not run? One of us might fall down and get hurt if we run.) Stress any special safety measures that apply to your school building.

Topical signs to be learned: October, fire, firefighter, 911, telephone, remember, keep, happen, help, remain calm, what do, never, safety.
Indicators: A.1.a, A.1.b, A.1.c, A.1.d, A.2.a, A.2.b, A.2.c, B.1.c, B.2.a, B.2.b, B.2.c, C.2.b, F.1.b, F.2.b, F.2.c, F.2.d, F.2.e, F.2.h, F.4.a, G.1.a, G.2.a, H.1.d, H.2.a.

Copyright © 2008 Time to Sign, Inc.

Community and School

Fire Safety (fire & police)
Materials: fire extinguisher, smoke alarm, rope ladder, fire stairway or exit

Discuss what to do in case of a fire. Show the children things in the room or building that are used in case of a fire. Point out fire extinguishers, smoke alarms, and fire exits. If applicable, show the children how to use a rope ladder. Discuss how a smoke alarm works and what we should do when one goes off. Go through a few practice fire drills, asking and answering questions, until the children understand exactly what they should do in case of a fire.

Topical signs to be learned: fire, what do, smoke, how, practice, remain calm, telephone, 911, firefighter, fire engine.
Indicators: A.1.a, A.1.b, A.1.c, A.1.d, A.2.a, A.2.b, A.2.c, B.1.c, B.2.a, B.2.b, B.2.c, C.2.b, F.1.b, F.2.b, F.2.c, F.2.d, F.2.e, F.2.h, F.4.a, G.1.a, G.2.a, H.1.d, H.2.a.

Fix-it-Shop (community, dramatic play)
Materials: sturdy work table, various tools (hammer, screw driver, pliers, ruler, wrenches, etc.), duct tape, masking tape, ruler, measuring tape, muffin tin with choices of nuts/bolts/nails/washers/screws, used or broken things to repair (adding machine, clock, coffee maker, computer, hairdryer, iron, locks, mixer, radio, tape recorder, telephone, toaster, toys, vacuum (with all electrical cords removed), work gloves.

Set up a sturdy work table that can be hammered and bumped. Arrange the work materials under the table, on a shelf, or on boxes on the floor. Let children begin working on things. Taking them apart is most of the fun, but sometimes they can go back together again too!

Topical signs to be learned: fix, shop (store), tools, work, gloves, broken, machine, cost, money, scissors, glue, table, sell, buy.
Indicators: A.1.a, A.1.b, A.1.c, A.1.d, A.2.a, A.2.b, A.2.c, B.1.c, B.2.a, B.2.b, B.2.c, C.2.b, E.3.a, F.1.b, F.2.a, F.2.b, F.2.c, F.2.d, F.2.e, F.2.f, F.2.g, F.3.a, F.3.b, F.3.c, F.4.b, F.4.c, G.1.a, G.1.b, G.2.a, G.3.a, H.1.a, H.1.b, H.1.d, H.2.a.

Germs and Doctors (health)
This game can have 10-50 players. This is a form of tag where there is one player chosen to be a germ for every 5 players and a player chosen to be a doctor for every 10. When the game starts, germs attempt to tag people, who then collapse on the ground (a crouch will suffice) and start calling out and signing "Doctor, doctor!" At this point, one of the players designated as a doctor can come to heal the sick with a touch. Of course, doctors can get sick, too, and need a doctor. If all the doctors get infected, no one can be cured any longer. The game goes on until the germs and everyone get tired or all players are infected. This is also not a bad way to show what happens with real illness, diseases, and doctor shortages.

Topical signs to be learned: doctor, sick, better, touch, real.
Indicators: A.1.a, A.1.b, A.1.c, A.1.d, A.2.a, A.2.b, A.2.c, B.1.c, B.2.a, B.2.b, B.2.c, C.2.b, F.1.b, F.2.b, F.2.c, F.2.d, F.2.e, F.2.h, F.3.c, G.1.a, G.2.a, H.1.d, H.2.a.

Copyright © 2008 Time to Sign, Inc.

Community and School

"I Know" Board (community)
Materials: bulletin board, cut our letters, children's pictures.

Have the children recite their full name, their parents/guardians names, their phone number and their address. Title the bulletin board "I know my....", you will have 4 separate lists "my full name", "my address", "my phone number", and "my parent/guardian's name". When the child can recite one of the following correctly, place their name on the board under the correct category.

Topical signs to be learned: name, mom, dad, telephone, number signs, address, know, my, say.
Indicators: A.1.c, A.1.d, A.2.a, A.2.b, A.2.c, B.1.c, B.2.a, B.2.b, B.3.a, B.5.b, B.5.c, C.2.b, F.1.b, F.2.b, F.2.c, F.2.d, F.2.e, F.2.h, F.3.c, F.4.a, F.5.a, G.1.a, G.2.a, H.1.a, H.1.b.

I Spy (school, colors, shapes)
Have the children sit in a circle. Teach or review colors and shapes. Have the children take turns, or raise their hands when they know the answer, finding items throughout the classroom when you give them the color and the shape of the item in sign. (Can also be played to other topical areas such as animals and transportation signs.)

Topical signs to be learned: colors, shapes, sit in circle, I, see, find.
Indicators: A.1.a, A.1.b, A.1.c, A.1.d, A.2.a, A.2.b, A.2.c, B.1.c, B.2.a, B.2.b, B.2.c, C.2.a, C.2.b, F.1.b, F.2.b, F.2.c, F.2.d, F.2.e, F.2.h, F.3.c, F.4.b, G.1.a, G.1.b, G.2.a, H.1.a, H.1.b, H.1.d.

It's My Job (occupations)
Materials: old magazines and catalogs, scissors, glue, index cards or lightweight cardboard cut into index cards.

Cut out pictures of different jobs and careers from magazines or catalogs and glue them onto index cards. Let dry.
Place the cards face down on the floor. Have 1-8 players sit around the cards in a circle. Player one looks at a card then places it face down so no one else can see it. Then he acts or mimes what the job on the card is like to them. The others try to guess what job they are acting out. Remove the card and the next person takes a turn acting out a job.

Topical signs to be learned: occupation signs, act, guess, work/job.
Indicators: A.1.a, A.1.b, A.1.c, A.1.d, A.2.a, A.2.b, A.2.c, B.1.c, B.2.a, B.2.b, B.2.c, C.2.b, E.3.a, F.1.b, F.2.b, F.2.c, F.2.d, F.2.e, F.2.h, F.3.c, G.1.a, G.1.b, G.2.a, H.1.a, H.1.b, H.1.d.

Lacing Cards (fire & police)
Materials: poster board, crayons, yarn, hole punch.

Cut colored poster board into badge shapes and punch holes around the edges. Have the children color their badges. Then lace yarn or a shoestring around the cards. (Can also make other shapes).

Topical signs to be learned: badge, string, color signs, crayon.

Copyright © 2008 Time to Sign, Inc.

Indicators: A.1.a, A.1.b, A.1.c, A.1.d, A.2.a, A.2.b, A.2.c, B.1.c, B.2.a, B.2.b, B.2.c, C.2.b, F.1.b, F.2.b, F.2.c, F.2.d, F.2.e, F.2.h, F.3.c, G.1.a, G.1.b, G.2.a, H.1.a, H.1.b, H.1.d.

Matching Game (health)
Materials: large piece of butcher block paper or poster board with dental or medical items on it and matching set of picture cards.

Place various pictures of items depicting how we keep our teeth healthy on a large piece of butcher block paper or poster board. Make a matching set of pictures on index cards. Use basic pictures such as a dentist, toothbrush, toothpaste, healthy foods, etc. Have children match cards to correct item on large paper.

Topical signs to be learned: teeth, picture, same, dentist, food signs, health signs.
Indicators: A.1.a, A.1.b, A.1.c, A.1.d, A.2.a, A.2.b, A.2.c, B.1.c, B.2.a, B.2.b, B.2.c, C.2.b, F.1.b, F.2.b, F.2.c, F.2.d, F.2.e, F.2.h, F.3.a, F.3.b, F.3.c, F.4.b, G.1.a, G.1.b, G.2.a, G.3.a, H.1.a, H.1.b, H.1.d, H.3.a, H.3.b.

My Neighborhood (community)
Materials: sand table or a large shallow pan filled with dirt, pipe cleaners, scissors, small wooden blocks, straw, toothpicks, small found objects from nature (small rocks, leaves, sticks, pinecones, feathers, etc) (optional), shoe box (optional).

Fill the sand table or pan with dirt. Cut pipe cleaners into one-inch sticks. Stand around the sand table (or rug if using a pan). Explain that the land on Earth gives us a place to live. Make a neighborhood in the sand! Take out the wooden blocks. These are houses. Each child chooses a house and places it on the land. Build roads! Take a straw and draw a road in the dirt. Plant trees! Pass out toothpicks. These are young trees that do not have any leaves. Each child chooses a tree and plants it in the dirt. Add people! Take out the cut pipe cleaners and stick a person in the neighborhood. If using nature objects add for rocks, buildings, trees, mountains etc. Look at the neighborhood. The Earth gives us a place to live!
You can have each child bring a shoe box from home to make a neighborhood. put dirt in the shoe boxes. Offer a variety of items. Make neighborhood scenes in the boxes, using the items on the table.

Topical signs to be learned: live, house, neighbor, people, street, tree.
Indicators: A.1.a, A.1.b, A.1.c, A.1.d, A.2.a, A.2.b, A.2.c, B.1.c, B.2.a, B.2.b, B.2.c, C.2.b, E.3.a, F.1.b, F.2.a, F.2.b, F.2.c, F.2.d, F.2.e, F.2.h, F.3.a, F.3.b, F.3.c, F.4.b, G.1.a, G.1.b, G.2.a, G.3.a, H.1.b, H.1.d.

Name Hunt (school)
Materials: paper, scissors, black felt pen, matching stickers, tape.

Cut 4"x8" strips of paper, one for each child. Print each child's name on one of the strips. Place a different sticker on each name strip. Tape the name strips around the room. Tell the children each one has their name hidden around the room and a sticker on their name. Give each child a sticker that matches their name strip. Go on a name hunt. Everyone looks for their name with the matching sticker. When a child finds their name,

Copyright © 2008 Time to Sign, Inc.

Community and School

they place their sticker on the name strip and bring it to the teacher. When all the name strips have been found, say each name and show the children as you say it. Fingerspell the names as you say them.

Topical signs to be learned: name, alphabet signs, hide, find, bring.
Indicators: A.1.a, A.1.b, A.1.c, A.1.d, A.2.a, A.2.b, A.2.c, B.1.c, B.2.a, B.2.b, B.2.c, B.5.a, B.5.b, B.5.c, C.2.b, F.1.b, F.2.a, F.2.b, F.2.c, F.2.d, F.2.e, F.2.h, F.3.c, F.4.b, G.1.a, G.1.b, G.2.a, H.1.a, H.1.b, H.1.d.

Neighborhood Map (lost, emergencies)
Materials: roll or butcher block paper, map, pencils/markers/crayons.

Have the children sit around a very large piece of paper (roll or butcher block). Show them a real map and how it is used. Have them each draw a part of the surrounding school/center area. Help them to make the map as real as possible. Talk about and point out where they should go in case of an emergency. Add 9-1-1 to the map. Add the nearest Police and Fire stations. Talk about the names of the roads surrounding your location. Sign them to better help the children remember them. Let them play with and add more features to their map. They can play with cars, trucks, figures, etc. Post on the wall when they are done or roll up for them to play with on another day.

Topical signs to be learned: house, friends, road, fingerspelling of names, 9-1-1, emergency, go, police, fire, road, car, truck.
Indicators: A.1.a, A.1.b, A.1.c, A.1.d, A.2.a, A.2.b, A.2.c, B.1.c, B.2.a, B.2.b, B.2.c, C.2.b, F.1.b, F.2.a, F.2.b, F.2.c, F.2.d, F.2.e, F.2.h, F.3.a, F.3.b, F.3.c, F.4.b, G.1.a, G.1.b, G.2.a, G.3.a, H.1.b, H.1.d.

Rescue (emergencies)
This is a very noisy game and should not be played if it is likely to bother neighbors or other classes.
One child is "It" and the rest can go anywhere in the area where the doors are open. As soon as "It" touches another player, that player has to stand still and shout for "Rescue!" He can't move until another player comes along and touches him, so the smart "It" hangs around and grabs the others as they attempt a rescue. The game ends when everyone except "It" is standing stock-still shouting for rescue!

Topical signs to be learned: door, open, touch, stand, still, shout, rescue (safety), can't, move, other.
Indicators: A.1.a, A.1.b, A.1.c, A.1.d, A.2.a, A.2.b, A.2.c, B.1.c, B.2.a, B.2.b, C.2.b, E.3.a, F.1.b, F.2.a, F.2.b, F.2.c, F.2.d, F.2.e, F.2.h, F.3.a, F.3.c, F.4.a, G.1.a, G.1.b, G.2.a, H.1.d, H.2.a.

Simon Says
Play Simon Says with a twist. Review basic signs and numbers needed to play the game Simon Says. Then give them instructions using ASL.

    Sample
    Simon Says touch toes

Copyright © 2008 Time to Sign, Inc.

Simon Says touch nose
Simon Says jump 3 times
Place hands on shoulders (eliminated)

Topical signs to be learned: say, touch, hands, face, jump, stop, spin, number signs, etc.
Indicators: A.1.a, A.1.b, A.1.c, A.1.d, A.2.a, A.2.b, A.2.c, B.1.c, B.2.a, B.2.b, C.2.b, F.1.b, F.2.a, F.2.b, F.2.c, F.2.d, F.2.e, F.2.h, F.3.c, F.4.b, G.1.a, G.1.b, G.2.a, H.1.a, H.1.b, H.1.d, H.2.a.

Smoke Crawl (fire & police)
Explain to the children that if there is a lot of smoke that they should crawl instead of walk. Have the children practice crawling.

Topical signs to be learned: smoke, walk, don't, down.
Indicators: A.1.a, A.1.b, A.1.c, A.1.d, A.2.a, A.2.b, A.2.c, B.1.c, B.2.a, B.2.b, B.2.c, C.2.b, F.1.b, F.2.a, F.2.b, F.2.c, F.2.d, F.2.e, F.2.h, F.4.a, G.1.a, G.2.a, H.1.d, H.2.a.

Telephone Smart (emergencies)
Materials: construction paper, marker, scissors.

Discuss using the telephone with children. Explain how using the telephone is for calling help. Introduce the emergency numbers in your area. Have the children practice saying the numbers. Explain children can dial "0" for the operator to receive help, as well. Use the following activities to help children remember the emergency numbers:
- Draw each number on large sheets of construction paper. Place the sheets on a paper on the rug about half an arm's length apart. Have the children jump from number to number, repeating the numbers out loud.
- Cut three small squares of paper. Print one number on each paper. Hide the squares around the room. Have the children hunt for the numbers and place them in order.
- Repeat the emergency numbers with the children three times in a row. Clap as you say each number. Have the children think of different ways to move as you say the numbers. They can march, twist, hope, or rock.

Topical signs to be learned: emergency, 9-1-1, telephone, help, jump, find, number signs.
Indicators: A.1.a, A.1.b, A.1.c, A.1.d, A.2.a, A.2.b, A.2.c, B.1.c, B.2.a, B.2.b, B.2.c, C.1.a, C.2.a, C.2.b, F.1.b, F.2.a, F.2.b, F.2.c, F.2.d, F.2.e, F.2.h, F.2.e, F.4.a, G.1.a, G.2.a, H.1.d.

Crafts

Art Shirts (school)
Materials: old adult size t-shirt from home, paints, brushes.

Have the children decorate an old t-shirt that they can use as a smock for future art projects. Help them to paint their name on it.

Topical signs to be learned: shirt, decorate, paint, color signs, name, alphabet signs, art.
Indicators: A.1.b, A.1.c, A.1.d, A.2.a, A.2.b, A.2.c, B.1.c, B.5.a, B.5.b, B.5.c, C.2.b, F.1.b, F.2.b, F.2.c, F.2.d, F.2.e, F.2.h, F.3.c, F.4.a., G.1.a, G.1.b, G.2.a, H.1.a, H.1.b, H.1.c, H.1.d.

Community and School

Big Clowns (health)
Materials: butcher paper, markers, paint and smocks.

Trace the children's bodies on a big piece of butcher paper. When you go around their heads add a clown hat. When you go around their necks add a big collar. When you go around their feet make big clown shoes. Have the children paint their own clown shape. Cut out and post throughout the room/hallway.

Topical signs to be learned: paint, clown, hat, scissors.
Indicators: A.1.b, A.1.c, A.1.d, A.2.a, A.2.b, A.2.c, B.1.c, B.2.a, C.2.b, F.1.a, F.1.b, F.2.b, F.2.c, F.2.d, F.2.e, F.2.h, F.3.c, F.4.a., G.1.a, G.1.b, G.2.a, H.1.a, H.1.b, H.1.c, H.1.d.

Bookmarks (school)
Materials: clear Con-Tact Paper®, old artwork, scissors, ruler, pencil.

Measure and mark back of artwork into rectangle(s) of bookmark size. (1 1/2 inch by 5 inches (4 by 12 cm) is a good size.) Cut out bookmark carefully. Cut out 2 rectangles of Con-Tact Paper for each bookmark that are 1/2 inch (1 cm) wider and longer. (2 inches by 5 1/2 inches or 5 by 13 cm) Remove backing from one piece of Con-Tact Paper and carefully center artwork rectangle on sticky side. Press down. Remove backing from the other piece of Con-Tact Paper and carefully place on other side of artwork, making a sandwich. Air bubbles can be smoothed out using the edge of the ruler. If the edges of the Con-Tact Paper are not even, they can be trimmed slightly after first drawing a new straight line as a guide.

Topical signs to be learned: book, scissors, draw,
Indicators: A.1.b, A.1.c, A.1.d, A.2.a, A.2.b, A.2.c, B.1.c, B.2.a, C.2.b, F.1.b, F.2.b, F.2.c, F.2.d, F.2.e, F.2.h, F.3.c, F.4.a., G.1.a, G.1.b, G.2.a, H.1.a, H.1.b, H.1.c, H.1.d.

Buttons and Bows Collage (school)
Materials: discarded buttons, fasteners, zippers, spools, bows, roll ends of trim, rickrack, lace, bias tape, ribbon, fabric (cloth, felt, fur, etc.), empty fabric board (heavy cardboard), glue (may need tacky glue to hold some items on surface), scissors.

Lay out materials in shallow containers or on the work surface. Give each child a piece of fabric board/cardboard. Allow children to choose items and glue them onto their board until they are finished.

Topical signs to be learned: choose, glue, finish.
Indicators: A.1.b, A.1.c, A.1.d, A.2.a, A.2.b, A.2.c, B.1.c, B.2.a, C.2.b, F.1.b, F.2.b, F.2.c, F.2.d, F.2.e, F.2.h, F.3.c, F.4.a., G.1.a, G.1.b, G.2.a, H.1.a, H.1.b, H.1.c, H.1.d.

Cityscape (community)
Materials: odds and ends of scrap lumber, dowels, pegs, toothpicks, large pieces of heavy cardboard (flattened packing box), glue, paint and brushes (optional), magazines (optional), scissors (optional).

This activity helps teach children about their own town or city by recreating it. Never mind if their model is not too accurate, or to scale, or not readily identifiable.

Copyright © 2008 Time to Sign, Inc.

Lay out cardboard on the ground. Arrange the scrap lumber to form buildings, roads, signs, cars. Glue your city onto the background. For older children, they may paint their buildings, put windows and doors. Pictures of buildings, vehicles, bridges, and the like may be cut out of magazines and mounted on the cityscape.

Topical signs to be learned: community signs, building, street, car, bridge.
Indicators: A.1.b, A.1.c, A.1.d, A.2.a, A.2.b, A.2.c, B.1.c, B.2.a, C.2.b, F.1.b, F.2.b, F.2.c, F.2.d, F.2.e, F.2.h, F.3.c, F.4.a., G.1.a, G.1.b, G.2.a, H.1.a, H.1.b, H.1.c, H.1.d.

Classroom Books (school)
Materials: Polaroid camera, film, magazines, crayons, paper.

Ideas that you might include are the following: name of child, birth date, mom and dad's names, sibling's names, pets they have, favorite toys they enjoy playing with, magazine cut outs of interests, space for a photo and a personal drawing. You can take a Polaroid photograph of each child to place on their page and let the children decide what information they would like to add.
One additional item you might wish to include would be a space in the back of the book for comments from the parents after they have viewed the book with their child.
Allow one child to take the book home on Monday and return it to class by Friday the same week. Share any personal comments that your parents have written in the book with the class when the book is returned.
Don't forget you are part of your classroom book as well; you must have a page like everyone else.

Topical signs to be learned: picture, book, name, birthday, family signs, alphabet, pet signs, favorite,
Indicators: A.1.b, A.1.c, A.1.d, A.2.a, A.2.b, A.2.c, B.1.a, B.1.b, B.1.c, B.1.d, B.2.a, B.2.b, B.3.a, B.3.b, B.4.a, B.5.a, B.5.b, C.2.b, F.1.a, F.1.b, F.2.b, F.2.c, F.2.d, F.2.e, F.2.h, F.3.c, F.4.a., F.5.a, G.1.a, G.1.b, G.2.a, H.1.a, H.1.b, H.1.c, H.1.d.

Classroom Tree (school, science & nature)
Materials: butcher paper, felt pen, markers or crayons, construction paper (optional), scissors (optional), glue (optional), paint (optional).

Draw a large tree on a sheet of butcher paper. Place the sheet on a table and have the children color it. The children can trace their hands on the tree for leaves or on construction paper and cut the handshapes out and glue them on the tree. Or make hand prints with paint on the tree. You can write children's names on their handprints or names and birthdays for a class birthday tree.

Topical signs to be learned: tree, leaves, crayon, hands, paper, scissors, glue, paint, name, birthday, color signs.
Indicators: A.1.b, A.1.c, A.1.d, A.2.a, A.2.b, A.2.c, B.1.c, B.2.a, B.2.b, C.2.b, F.1.a, F.1.b, F.2.b, F.2.c, F.2.d, F.2.e, F.2.h, F.3.c, F.4.a., G.1.a, G.1.b, G.2.a, H.1.b, H.1.c, H.1.d.

Firefighter Hats (fire & police)
Materials: newspaper or butcher paper, red paint, brushes, smocks.

Community and School  25

Make hats from newsprint or butcher paper. An easy way to do this is to place the paper on the child's head, then place a piece of masking tape around the paper like a headband while it's on the child's head. Then crumple the sides up. Have the children paint their hats red.

Topical signs to be learned: hat, paper, paint, red.
Indicators: A.1.b, A.1.c, A.1.d, A.2.a, A.2.b, A.2.c, B.1.c, B.2.a, C.2.b, F.1.b, F.2.b, F.2.c, F.2.d, F.2.e, F.2.h, F.3.c, F.4.a., G.1.a, G.1.b, G.2.a, H.1.b, H.1.c, H.1.d.

Fire Engine (fire & police)
Materials: construction paper, scissors, yarn, straws.

Precut circular and rectangular shapes from construction paper. Have the children glue the precut shapes on to a piece of construction paper to resemble a fire truck. They may add yarn or string for the fire hose and use straws to make a ladder.

Topical signs to be learned: triangle, rectangle, glue, fire truck, fire.
Indicators: A.1.b, A.1.c, A.1.d, A.2.a, A.2.b, A.2.c, B.1.c, B.2.a, C.2.b, F.1.b, F.2.b, F.2.c, F.2.d, F.2.e, F.2.h, F.3.c, F.4.a., G.1.a, G.1.b, G.2.a, H.1.b, H.1.c, H.1.d.

Fire Painting (fire & police)
Materials: red paint, orange paint, black paint, paper, plastic wrap, squeegee, cut out of a house.

Using colors associated with fire (red, orange) squirt or draw thick lines on a piece of paper and add a few drops of black paint here and there. Press clear plastic wrap onto the paper and squeegee the paint around. Pull plastic off of the paper using a strong vertical pulling action. (This will cause the paint to look like fire.) When paint is dry have the children glue a black cutout of a house (windows cut out) and/or a black cutout of a fire truck.

Topical signs to be learned: red, orange, fire, paper, house, fire truck, glue.
Indicators: A.1.b, A.1.c, A.1.d, A.2.a, A.2.b, A.2.c, B.1.c, B.2.a, C.2.b, F.1.b, F.2.b, F.2.c, F.2.d, F.2.e, F.2.h, F.3.c, F.4.a., G.1.a, G.1.b, G.2.a, H.1.b, H.1.c, H.1.d.

I Love You (ILU) Impressions - Handprint (intro to sign language, gifts)
Read the Kissing Hand. Then using "ILU" handsign the children can make gifts for their parents or others, by making handprint impressions in clay. Once clay is hard, the children can then paint their "ILU" hand-prints.

Materials: clay, paint, paintbrushes and smocks.
Indicators: A.1.b, A.1.c, A.1.d, A.2.a, A.2.b, A.2.c, B.1.c, B.2.a, C.2.b, F.1.b, F.2.b, F.2.c, F.2.d, F.2.e, F.2.h, F.3.c, F.4.a., G.1.a, G.1.b, G.2.a, H.1.a, H.1.b, H.1.c, H.1.d.

Magazine and Starch Collage (school)
Materials: old magazines and catalogs, scissors, liquid starch in small container (less messy than glue), wide paintbrush, paper or cardboard (about 18" x 24").

Have each child decide on a theme for their collage such as things I like to do, jungle

Copyright © 2008 Time to Sign, Inc.

animals, etc. Or give children a theme. Give magazines and catalogs to children and have them cut or tear out pictures they want for their collage. With wide paintbrush, paint liquid starch over the area to be covered by a picture or on back of picture. Lay picture down and paint more starch over it (it will dry clear). Allow finished collages to dry flat before hanging or mounting for display.

Topical signs to be learned: scissors, glue, picture, dry.
Indicators: A.1.b, A.1.c, A.1.d, A.2.a, A.2.b, A.2.c, B.1.c, B.2.a, C.2.b, F.1.b, F.2.b, F.2.c, F.2.d, F.2.e, F.2.h, F.3.c, F.4.a., G.1.a, G.1.b, G.2.a, H.1.b, H.1.c, H.1.d.

Police Badges (fire & police)
Materials: poster board, aluminum foil.
Supply the children with tag board in the shape of a badge. Have them wrap tin foil around the badge to make a police badge.

Topical signs to be learned: police/badge, silver.
Indicators: A.1.b, A.1.c, A.1.d, A.2.a, A.2.b, A.2.c, B.1.c, B.2.a, C.2.b, F.1.b, F.2.b, F.2.c, F.2.d, F.2.e, F.2.h, F.3.c, F.4.a., G.1.a, G.1.b, G.2.a, H.1.b, H.1.c, H.1.d.

Postcards and Stamps (mail)
Materials: plain white paper, 1 package unflavored gelatin, 2 tablespoons of any fruit juice, saucepan, brush, ruler, paper for postcards such as heavy paper, old greeting cards, wrapping paper, magazine clippings, photos, or index cards; colored pencils, crayons, markers, or pens, scissors, glue/tape/paste, materials for dress-up play (optional), letter carrier hat (any suitable dress-up hat), letter carrier shoulder delivery bag (old purse), *Never Mail an Elephant* by Mike Thaler.

Read the book *Never Mail an Elephant* by Mike Thaler about the process of preparing and sending mail in a delightfully funny way. The narrator has trouble mailing an elephant as a birthday present to cousin Edna. First make a sheet of pretend stamps. Fold a piece of plain white paper into squares. Any size is fine, stamp size or larger. Draw or color a picture in each box. For most authentic stamps, write a number on the stamp that tells how much it is worth. Set aside until the stamp glue is ready.
Make the glue for lickable stamps. Mix the gelatin and fruit juice in a small saucepan and heat. When cool, brush the glue on the back of a sheet of paper designed as stamps. Let dry. Cut the stamps apart on the folded lines. Set aside until the postcards are ready or use to "mail" other letters. Prepare postcards to pretend-mail. Use any heavy paper cut into card shapes, or use index cards. Decorate one side of the postcard with drawings, magazine clippings, photographs, wrapping paper, or other ideas. Then turn the card over. Write a message and also the name of the person to whom it is being mailed. Lick and stick on a stamp. Place the card in a pretend delivery bag, and deliver to the person for whom it is intended.

Topical signs to be learned: mail, stamp, letter, mail carrier, paper, pencil, crayon, scissors, glue, hat, elephant, never, mail box, post office, write.
Indicators: A.1.b, A.1.c, A.1.d, A.2.a, A.2.b, A.2.c, B.1.c, B.2.a, C.2.b, F.1.b, F.2.b, F.2.c, F.2.d, F.2.e, F.2.h, F.3.c, F.4.a., G.1.a, G.1.b, G.2.a, H.1.b, H.1.c, H.1.d.

Community and School

Real-People Paper Dolls
Materials: a large roll of strong paper at least 36 inches wide, crayons, markers, colored pencils or paints, felt-tip pens, scissors, tape.

Have one child lie down on a large sheet of paper (big enough to surround the entire body). With a felt-tip pen, trace the child's outline on the paper. Help the child personalize the outline by drawing in and coloring hair, facial features, and clothing. Repeat for the others in the group. Discuss specific body parts with the children. Have children identify their own and other children's body parts on their cutouts. Write each child's name on his/her drawing; cut it out along the outline and tape it to the child's back or the wall.

Topical signs to be learned: head, hands, (for other body parts, point to the part), crayon, paint, pencil, scissors, color signs.
Indicators: A.1.b, A.1.c, A.1.d, A.2.a, A.2.b, A.2.c, B.1.c, B.2.a, C.2.b, F.1.b, F.2.b, F.2.c, F.2.d, F.2.e, F.2.h, F.3.c, F.4.a., G.1.a, G.1.b, G.2.a, H.1.b, H.1.c, H.1.d.

Tooth (dentist, dental hygiene)
Materials: pre-cut shape of a tooth for each child, paint or toothpaste, toothbrushes, water (if toothpaste is used) and smocks.

Paint precut tooth shape with real toothbrushes.
Indicators: A.1.b, A.1.c, A.1.d, A.2.a, A.2.b, A.2.c, B.1.c, B.2.a, C.2.b, F.1.b, F.2.b, F.2.c, F.2.d, F.2.e, F.2.h, F.3.c, F.4.a., G.1.a, G.1.b, G.2.a, H.1.b, H.1.c, H.1.d.

Copyright © 2008 Time to Sign, Inc.

Community Signs

-

Señales en la Comunidad

Community and School  29

Insert the dominant flattened "O" handshape, palm facing up, into the reference "C" handshape, palm facing forward, with a double movement.

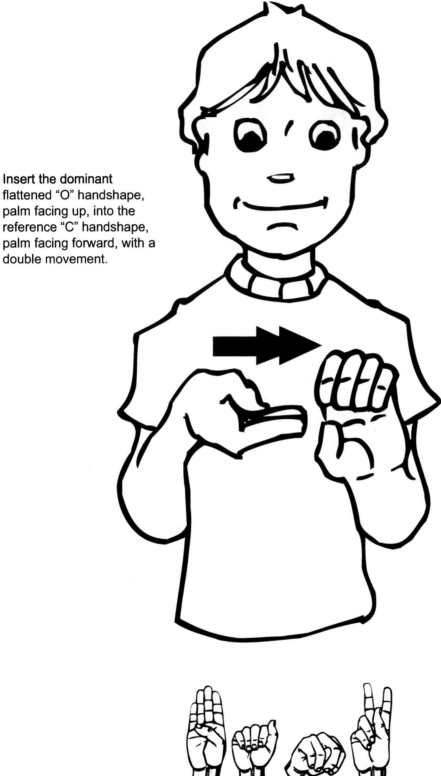

bank – banco

Community and School

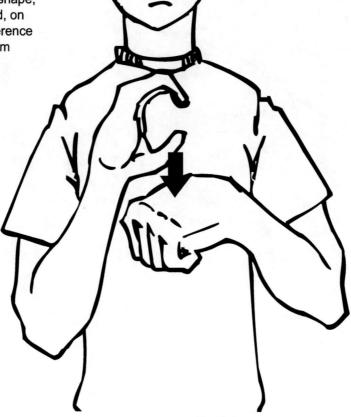

Tap the thumb of the dominant "C" handshape, palm facing forward, on the back of the reference "S" handshape, palm facing down.

church - iglesia

Copyright © 2008 Time to Sign, Inc.

Community and School  31

Hook the dominant "X" handshape index finger with the index finger of the upturned reference "X" handshape, then reverse this same movement.

[As if holding hands with **someone**]

[Hooking just once without flipping hands in reverse and re-hooking means "best friends"]

friend – amigo

Copyright © 2008 Time to Sign, Inc.

Community and School

Move the dominant "L" handshape, palm facing forward, in a circle in front of the dominant shoulder.

library - biblioteca

Community and School

Bring the back of the dominant bent hand from the chest forward towards the reference bent hand, both palms facing in, and fingers pointing in opposite directions. Next, start with the fingertips of both open ands touching, palms angled towards each other, bring the hands at a downward angle outward in front of each should straight down, ending with the fingertips pointing up and the palms facing each other. Then move both open hands, palm facing each other, downward along each side of the body.

[Sign: near + house + agent]

neighbor – vecino

Copyright © 2008 Time to Sign, Inc.

Community and School

Move the dominant "P" handshape, palm facing down, in a large circular movement over the bent reference arm, palm facing down and held across the body.

park - parque

Community and School  35

Touch the fingers of the dominant "R" handshape, palm facing in, first to the dominant side and then to the reference side of the chin.

restaurant – restaurante

Copyright © 2008 Time to Sign, Inc.

Start with both flattened "O" handshapes in front of each side of the body, palms and fingers facing down, swing the fingers forward and back from the wrist with a repeated movement.

store – tienda

Community and School

Fire & Police Signs - Señales de Incendio y Policía

Move the dominant "A" handshape, palm facing in, first downward a short distance on the upper reference arm and then across the back to front forming a plus sign.

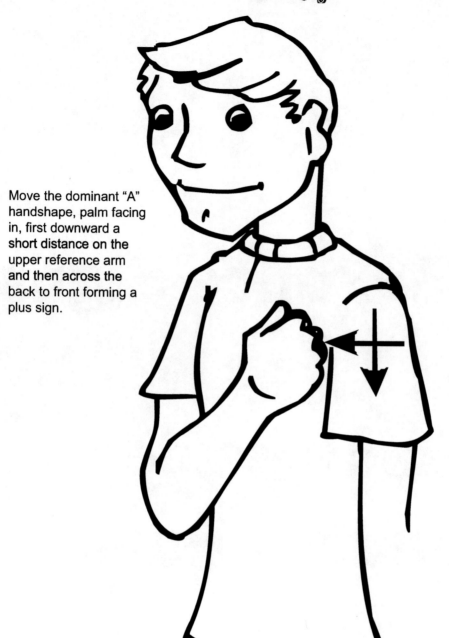

ambulance – ambulancia

Community and School  39

Tap the thumb side of the dominant modified "C" handshape against the reference side of the chest with a double movement.

[Indicates the badge]

badge – insignia

Copyright © 2008 Time to Sign, Inc.

Community and School

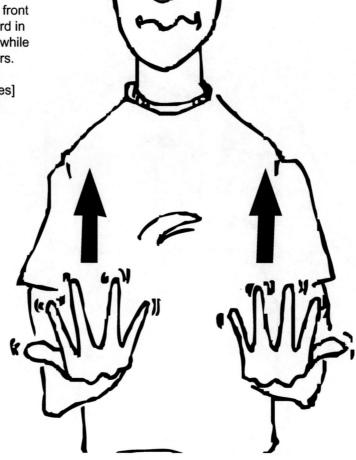

Move both "5" handshapes, palms facing up, from in front of the waist upward in front of the chest while wiggling the fingers.

[Represents flames]

fire – fuego

Community and School  41

Bring the back of the dominant "B" handshape, fingers pointing up and palm facing forward, against the center of the forehead.

[Represents the raised front of the firefighter's helmet]

firefighter - bombero

Copyright © 2008 Time to Sign, Inc.

Move both "5" handshapes, palm facing up from in front of the waist, upward in front of the chest and wiggle fingers. Then place the little finger side of the dominant "T" handshape touching the index finger side of the reference "T" handshape, palms facing opposite directions, move the dominant hand in while moving the reference hand out.

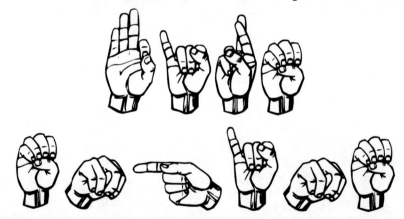

fire engine (truck) – camión de bomberos

Community and School  43

Place the open reference hand, palm facing upward, under the dominant "A" handshape, thumbs up, lift both hands together.

[Also: aid, assist]

help – ayuda

Copyright © 2008 Time to Sign, Inc.

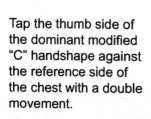

Tap the thumb side of the dominant modified "C" handshape against the reference side of the chest with a double movement.

[Indicates the badge]

police badge – insignia de Policiá

Community and School  45

Start with both "S" handshapes crossed at the wrists in front of the chest, palms facing opposite directions, twist the wrists and move the hands apart, ending with hands in front of each shoulder, palms facing forward.

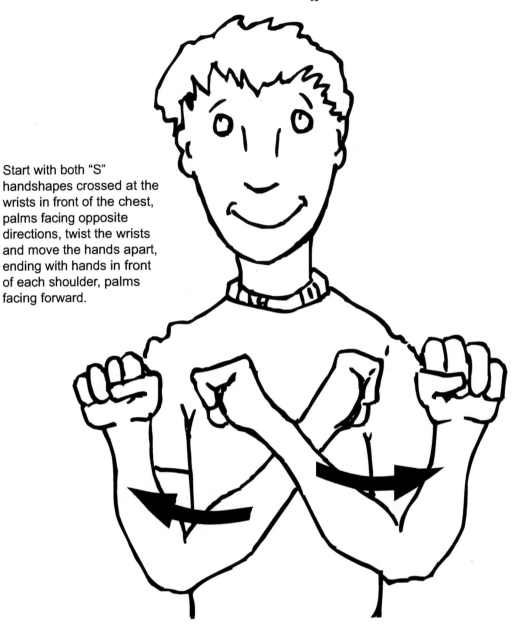

safety – seguro

Copyright © 2008 Time to Sign, Inc.

Mail Signs - Señales De Correo

Community and School 47

Move both "A" handshapes, palms facing in and held in front of the waist, upwards simultaneously.

address - dirección

Touch the extended thumb of the dominant "10" handshape to the lips, palm facing in, then move the thumb downward and touch the fingertips of the open reference hand held in front of the body, palm facing up.

[As if placing a stamp on a letter]

[Also: mail]

letter/mail - carta

Community and School 49

Touch the extended thumb of the dominant "10" handshape to the lips, palm facing in, then move the thumb downward and touch the fingertips of the open reference hand held in front of the body, palm facing up. Next with both open hands in front of each of the body, palms facing each other, fingers facing forward, move the hand in opposite direction, ending with the reference hand near the chest and the dominant several inches forward of the reference hand, both palms facing in.

mailbox - buzón

Copyright © 2008 Time to Sign, Inc.

Touch the extended thumb of the dominant "10" handshape to the lips, palm facing in, then move the thumb downward and touch the fingertips of the open reference hand held in front of the body, palm facing up. Then start with both open handshapes facing each other at shoulder height, move both hands down simultaneously.

[Sign: mail + agent]

mail carrier - ofocina de cartero

Community and School

Fingerspell the letters "P" and "O".

post office- oficina de correos

Community and School

Touch the extended dominant "U" handshape to the lips, palm facing in, then move the "U" handshape downward and touch the fingertips of the open reference hand held in front of the body, palm facing up.

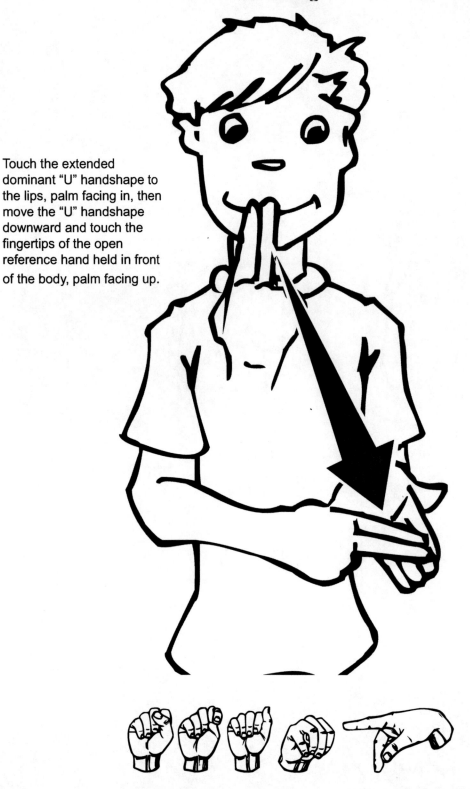

stamp - sello

Community and School

Bring the finger of the dominant modified "X" handshape, palm facing towards reference hand, with a wiggly movement from the heel to the fingers of the open referenced hand held in front of the body palm facing up.

write – escribir

Health Care Signs

-

Señales De Servicios Médicos

Community and School

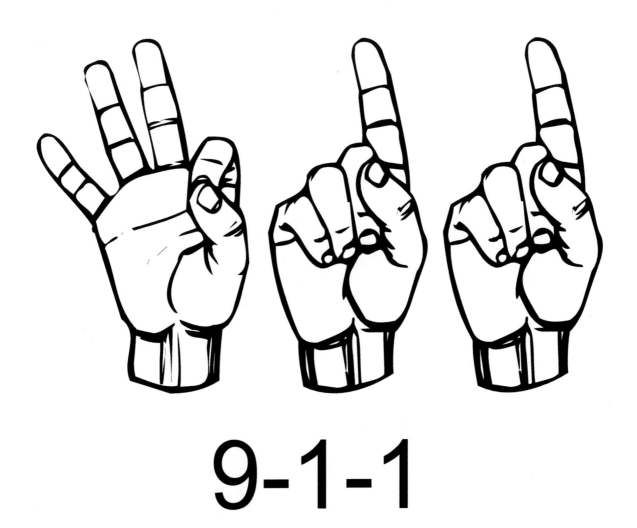

9-1-1

Display "9" handshape, then "1" handshape, then another "1" handshape.

Community and School

Bring the dominant open hand, palm facing in, from in front of the mouth upward in an arc changing to a "10" handshape as the hand moves.

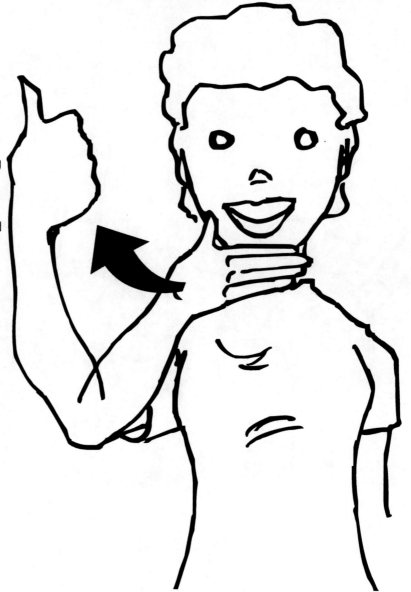

better - mejor

Community and School  57

Touch the fingers of both open hands, palms facing in and fingers pointing towards each other, first on each side of the chest and then on teach side of he waist with both hands simultaneously.

body - cuerpo

Copyright © 2008 Time to Sign, Inc.

58   **Community and School**

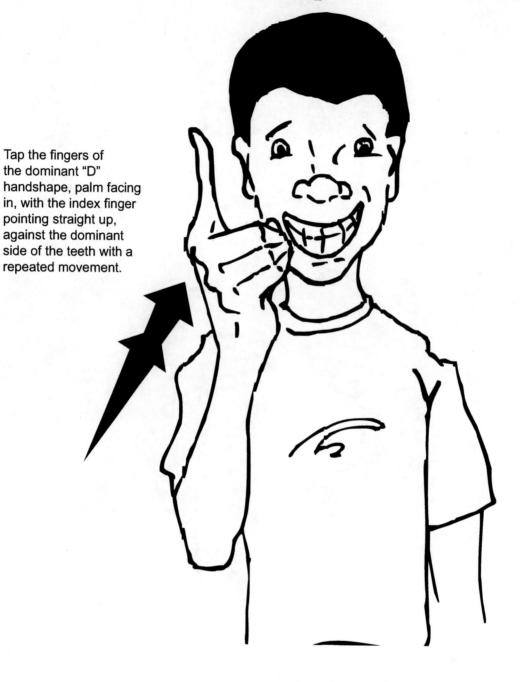

Tap the fingers of the dominant "D" handshape, palm facing in, with the index finger pointing straight up, against the dominant side of the teeth with a repeated movement.

dentist - dentista

Copyright © 2008 Time to Sign, Inc.

Community and School  59

Tap the extended fingers of the dominant "M" handshape, palm facing down, with a double movement of the wrist of the reference open hand held in front of the body, palm facing up.

[As if checking your pulse]

[Can also use the "D" handshape]

doctor - doctor

Copyright © 2008 Time to Sign, Inc.

Community and School

Brush the extended middle finger of the dominant "5" handshape, palm facing in, up the middle of the chest with a repeated movement.

feel - sentirse

Copyright © 2008 Time to Sign, Inc.

Community and School  61

Place the fingertips of the dominant bent hand against the dominant temple, palm facing down, and move downward in an arc until the fingertips touch the jaw line.

head - cabeza

Copyright © 2008 Time to Sign, Inc.

Bring the fingers of the dominant "H" handshape, palm facing in, first down a short distance on the upper reference arm and then across from back to front, creating a "plus sign"

hospital – hospital

Community and School 63

Begin with the index fingers pointing towards each other in front of the chest, palms facing in, jab the fingers toward each other with short repeated movement.

[Also: ache]

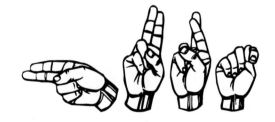

hurt - herido

Copyright © 2008 Time to Sign, Inc.

Tap the extended fingers of the dominant "N" handshape, palm facing down, with a double movement of the wrist of the reference open hand held in front of the body, palm facing up.

[As if checking your pulse]

nurse - enfermera

Community and School

65

Touch the bent middle finger of the dominant "5" handshape to the forehead while touching the bent index-finger of the reference "5" handshape to the chest, palms facing in.

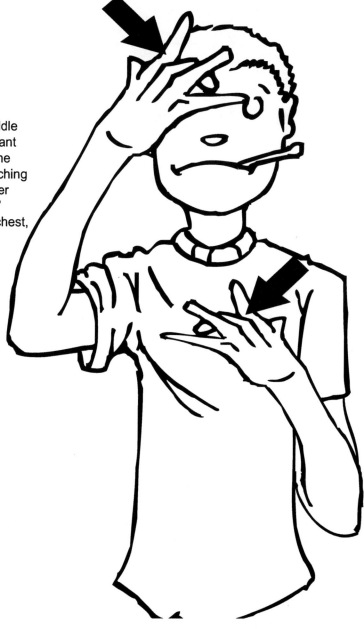

sick - enfermo

Copyright © 2008 Time to Sign, Inc.

Move the curved index-finger of the dominant "X" handshape in front of the teeth from the dominant to the reference side.

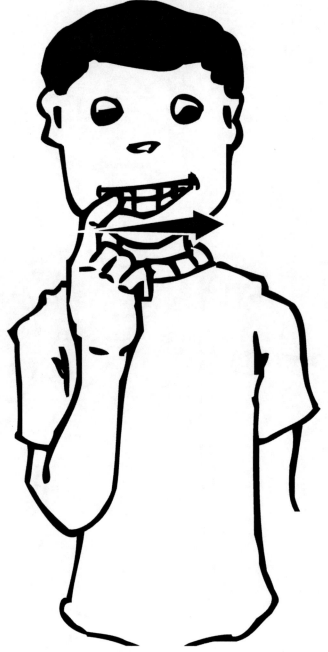

teeth - diente

Construction Signs - Señales De Construcción

Start with the fingers of the dominant bent hand overlapping the fingers of the reference bent hand in front of the chest, palms facing down; reverse the position of the hands with a repeated movement as they move up.

[As if making layers or "floors" on top of each other]

build – construir

Community and School  69

Start with both flattened "O" handshapes, palm facing up, in front of either side of the body, move the thumb of each hand smoothly across each fingertip, starting with the little fingers and ending as "A'" handshapes.

dirt – tierra

Copyright © 2008 Time to Sign, Inc.

Community and School

Start with both flattened "O" handshapes in front of the reference side of the body, palms facing down, move the hands in large arcs to the dominant side.

[As if moving an item from one side to the other]

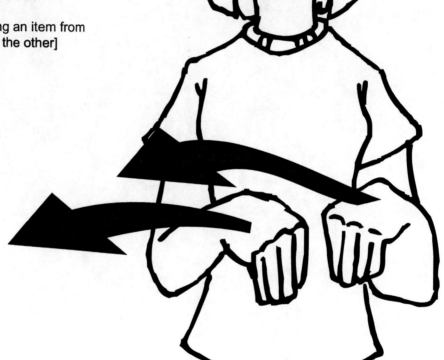

move- mover(se)

Community and School 71

Bring the "T" handshape of the dominant hand, palm facing up, and knuckles pointing forward, from the dominant side of the body in several large arcs outward.

[Or sign can be fingerspelled]

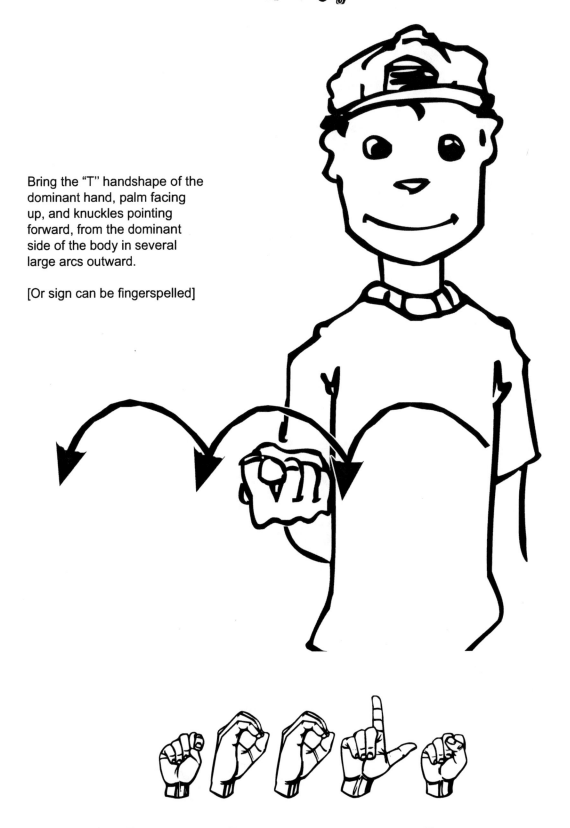

tools - herramientas

Copyright © 2008 Time to Sign, Inc.

Community and School

Start with the little-finger side of the dominant "T" handshape touching the index-finger side of the reference "T" handshape, palms facing opposite directions, move the dominant hand back towards the body while moving the reference hand out away from the body.

truck – camion

Occupation Signs

Señales De Ocupación

Move the fingertips of the dominant "F" hand, palm facing down, across the palm of the open reference hand, palm facing up from the heel to the fingers of the hand. Then move both open hands, palms facing each other, fingers pointing forward, downward from the chest to the waist simultaneously.

[Sign: count + agent]

accountant – contador

Community and School 75

Bring the thumbs of both "A" handshapes, palms facing each other, down each side of the chest with alternating circular movements. Then move both open hands, palms facing each other, fingers pointing forward, downward from the chest to the waist simultaneously.

[Sign: act + agent]

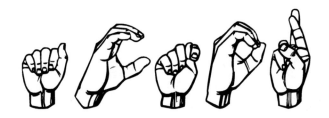

actor – actor

Community and School

Begin with both "A" handshapes touching, palms angled down, move them apart outward and then down, ending with palms facing each other. Then move both open hands, palms facing each other, fingers pointing forward, downward from the chest to the waist simultaneously.

architect –arquitecto

Copyright © 2008 Time to Sign, Inc.

Community and School

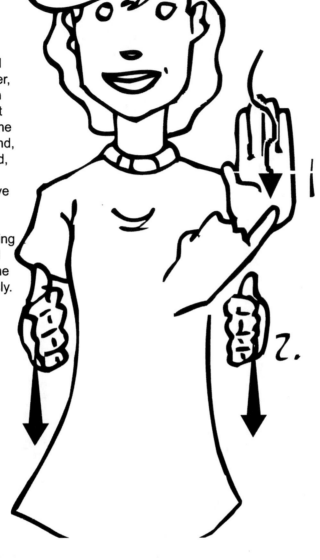

Move the extended dominant little finger, palm facing in, with a wiggly movement down the palm of the reference open hand, palm facing forward, from the fingers to the heel. Then move both open hands, palms facing each other, fingers pointing forward, downward from the chest to the waist simultaneously.

[Sign: art + agent]

artist – artista

Community and School

Begin with "A" handshapes touching, palms facing forward, move the dominant handshape upward and sideways in an arc.

astronaut – astronauta

Copyright © 2008 Time to Sign, Inc.

Community and School  79

Begin with the reference open hand, palm facing down and fingers pointing to dominant side, held in front of the reference side of chest, move the dominant flattened "O" handshape, palm facing up, forwards then backwards under the reference hand. Then move both open hands, palms facing each other, fingers pointing forward, downward from the chest to the waist simultaneously.

[Sign: bake + agent]

baker – panadero

Community and School

Insert the dominant flattened "O" handshape, palm facing up, into the reference "C" handshape, palm facing forward, with a double movement. Then move both open hands, palms facing each other, fingers pointing forward, downward from the chest to the waist simultaneously.

[Sign: bank + agent]

banker – banquero

Community and School

Begin with dominant "V" handshape at dominant side of forehead, palm facing body, move across the forehead towards the reference side while opening and closing the middle and ring fingers of the hand. Then move both open hands, palms facing each other, fingers pointing forward, downward from the chest to the waist simultaneously.

[Sign: haircut + agent]

barber – peluquero

Community and School

Tap the fingertips of the dominant curved "5" handshape on the dominant shoulder with a repeated movement, palm facing down.

[Also: boss, chieff]

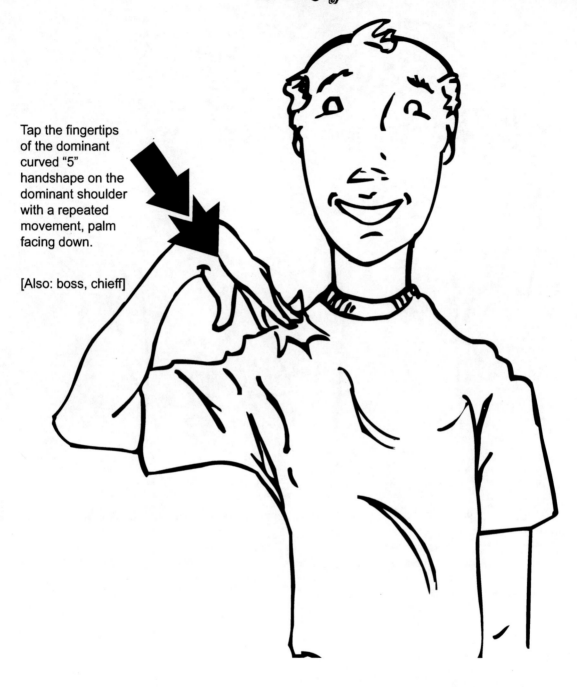

captain – capitán

Community and School

Begin with the little finger side of the dominant "K" handshape across the index finger side of the reference "K" handshape, palms facing in opposite directions, move the hands in a repeated flat circle in front of the body. Then move both open hands, palms facing each other, fingers pointing forward, downward from the chest to the waist simultaneously.

[Sign: care + agent]

caregiver - cuidadora(o)

Move both "S" handshapes, palms facing in, from reference to dominant side and back in front of body (as if sawing wood). Then move both open hands, palms facing each other, fingers pointing forward, downward from the chest to the waist simultaneously.

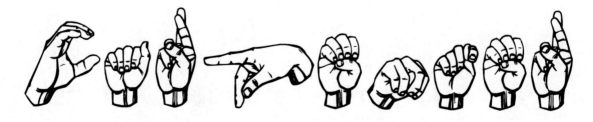

carpenter – carpintero

Community and School

Begin by moving the dominant open hand, palm facing down, from in front of the dominant shoulder downward with a repeated movement while wiggling the fingers. Then move both open hands, palms facing each other, fingers pointing forward, downward from the chest to the waist simultaneously.

[Sign: cash register + agent]

cashier –cajero

Begin by moving the thumb side of the dominant "C" handshape, palm facing reference side, from touching the lower part of the extended reference arm upward to touch the upper arm. Then move both open hands, palms facing each other, fingers pointing forward, downward from the chest to the waist simultaneously.
[Sign: computer + agent]

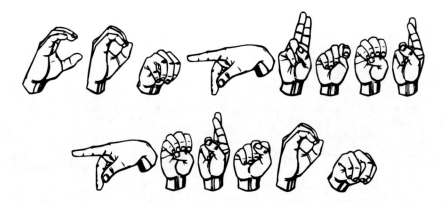

computer person –programador

Community and School

Push the little finger side of the dominant open hand, palm facing reference side, across the back of the reference open hand, palm facing down. Then move both "5" handshapes from in front of each side of the body, palms facing each other, forward with a parallel movement. Next, tap the fingertips of the dominant curved "5" handshape, palm facing down, on the dominant shoulder with a repeated movement.

[Sign: cross + street + officer]

crossing guard –
agente de transito escolar

Copyright © 2008 Time to Sign, Inc.

Community and School

With the thumbs of both "Y" handshapes touching in front of the chest, dominant palm facing forward and reference palm facing body, twist the hands in opposite directions with a double movement.

engineer – ingeniero

Copyright © 2008 Time to Sign, Inc.

Community and School  89

Touch the fingertips of the dominant flattened "O" handshape, palm facing body, first to the dominant side of the nose then to the reference side. Then move both open hands, palms facing each other, fingers pointing forward, downward from the chest to the waist simultaneously.

[Sign: flower + agent]

florist –florista

Copyright © 2008 Time to Sign, Inc.

Beginning with the bent dominant elbow resting on top of the back of the reference hand held across of the body, palm facing down; twist the dominant "5" handshape forward with

a double movement, moving the arms to the dominant side each time. Then move both open hands, palms facing each other, fingers pointing forward, downward from the chest to the waist simultaneously.

[Sign: forest + agent]

forester – guarda bosques

Community and School  91

Move the dominant "H" handshape, palm facing reference side, downward with a double movement in front of the dominant side of the body. Then move both open hands, palms facing each other, fingers pointing forward, downward from the chest to the waist simultaneously.

[Sign: history + agent]

historian – historiador

Copyright © 2008 Time to Sign, Inc.

Begin with the fingertips of both "F" handshapes touching in front of the chest, palms facing each other, twist the hands in the opposite directions to reverse positions. Then move both open hands, palms facing each other, fingers pointing forward, downward from the chest to the waist simultaneously.

[Sign: interpret + agent]

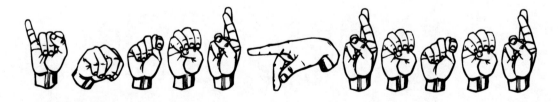

interpreter – intérprete

Community and School

Move the dominant modified "C" handshape, palm facing in, down the palm of the reference open hand, palm facing forward, from the fingers to the heel with a double

movement. Then move both open hands, palms facing each other, fingers pointing forward, downward from the chest to the waist simultaneously.

[Sign: article + agent]

journalist – periodista

Move both "F" handshapes, palms facing each other, up and down in front of each side of the chest with a repeated alternating movement. Then move both open hands, palms facing each other, fingers pointing forward, downward from the chest to the waist simultaneously.

[Sign: judge + agent]

judge – juez

Community and School

Place the palm side of the dominant "L" handshape, palm facing reference, first on the fingers then on the heel of the reference open hand, palm facing dominant side and fingers pointing up. Then move both open hands, palms facing each other, fingers pointing forward, downward from the chest to the waist simultaneously.

[Sign: law + agent]

lawyer – abogado

Move the dominant "L" handshape, palm facing forward, in a counterclockwise circle in front of dominant shoulder. Then move both open hands, palms facing each other, fingers pointing forward, downward from the chest to the waist simultaneously.

[Sign: library + agent]

librarian – bibliotecario

Community and School

Bring the fingertips of the dominant open handshape down the length of the reference hand palm with a double movement, pulling the back of the dominant hand fingers up the reference hand palm to the fingertips each time. Then move both open hands, palms facing each other, fingers pointing forward, downward from the chest to the waist simultaneously.

[Sign: paint + agent]

painter – pintor

Move the dominant "P" handshape, palm facing down, in a large circular movement over the bent reference arm, palm facing down and held across the body. Then tap the dominant modified "C" handshape, palm facing reference side, against the reference side of the chest in a double movement.

[Sign: park + police]

park ranger – policía de parques

Community and School  99

Begin with the dominant "F" handshape, palm facing forward, by the dominant side of the head, move the hand downward from the wrist with a double movement. Then move both open hands, palms facing each other, fingers pointing forward, downward from the chest to the waist simultaneously.

[Sign: preach + agent]

pastor – pastor religioso

Copyright © 2008 Time to Sign, Inc.

Fingerspell "P" then "E". Then move both flattened "O" handshapes, forward with a small double movement in front of each side of the head. Then start with both open handshapes facing each other at shoulder height, move both hands down simultaneously.

[Sign: finger spell "P" + "E" + teach + agent]

p.e. teacher – maestro de educación física

Community and School

Begin by moving the dominant "C" handshape, palm facing forward, from near the dominant side of the face downward, ending with the dominant "C" handshape against the palm of the reference open hand, palm facing dominant side. Then move both open hands, palms facing each other, fingers pointing forward, downward from the chest to the waist simultaneously.

[Sign: photo + agent]

photographer – fotógrafo

Copyright © 2008 Time to Sign, Inc.

Begin by moving the dominant hand with the thumb, index finger, and little finger extended, palm facing down, forward with a short repeated movement in front of the dominant shoulder. Then move both open hands, palms facing each other, fingers pointing forward, downward from the chest to the waist simultaneously.

[Sign: airplane + agent]

pilot –piloto

Community and School

Begin with the dominant "P" handshape near the dominant side of the forehead, palm facing forward, twist the wrist to turn the palm back and touch the middle finger of the dominant "P" handshape against the dominant side of the head. Then move both open hands, palms facing each other, fingers pointing forward, downward from the chest to the waist simultaneously.

[Sign: politics + agent]

politician – político

Begin with both "C" handshapes near the side of the forehead, palms facing forward, move the hands outward to above each shoulder while closing into "S" handshapes.

president – presidente

Community and School

Move the dominant "P" handshape, palm facing down, in a small circle above the reference open hand, palm facing down, ending with the middle finger of the dominant hand on the back of the reference hand.

principal – principal

Bring the fingers of the dominant modified "X" handshape, palm facing reference side, with a wiggly movement from the heel to the fingers of the reference open hand held in front of the body, palm facing up. Then move both open hands, palms facing each other, fingers pointing forward, downward from the chest to the waist simultaneously.

[Sign: write + agent]

reporter - reportero

Community and School  107

Begin with the dominant "10" handshape in front of the dominant shoulder and the reference "10" handshape in front of the reference shoulder, both palms facing forward, move the hands in large alternating circles toward each other. Then move both open hands, palms facing each other, fingers pointing forward, downward from the chest to the waist simultaneously.

[Sign: science + agent]

scientist - científico

Copyright © 2008 Time to Sign, Inc.

Bring the dominant modified "X" handshape from near the dominant side of the chin downward across the palm of the reference open hand from the heel to off the fingertips.

[The hand takes the words from the mouth and puts them on paper]

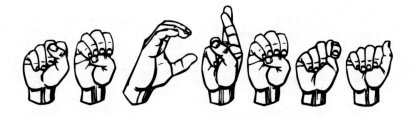

secretary – secretario(a)

Community and School

Move the dominant open "5" handshape, palm facing in, back and forth with a double movement across the length of the bent reference forearm held in front of the body, palm facing up. Then move both open hands, palms facing each other, fingers pointing forward, downward from the chest to the waist simultaneously.

[Sign: music + agent]

singer/musician – cantante, músico

Fingerspell the word "VET".

veterinarian- veterinario

Community and School

Pinch a small amount of clothing on the dominant side of the chest with the fingers of the dominant "F" handshape and pull forward with a short double movement. Then move both open hands, palms facing each other, fingers pointing forward, downward from the chest to the waist simultaneously.

[Sign: volunteer + agent]

volunteer – voluntario

Starting with the fingertips of both curved "5" handshapes on the chest near each shoulder, roll the fingers towards each other on their knuckles with a double movement while keeping the fingers in place. Begin with the dominant "10" handshape in front of the dominant shoulder and the reference "10" handshape in front of the reference shoulder, both palms facing forward, move the hands in large alternating circles toward each other. Then move both open hands, palms facing each other, fingers pointing forward, downward from the chest to the waist simultaneously.

[Sign: animal + science + agent]

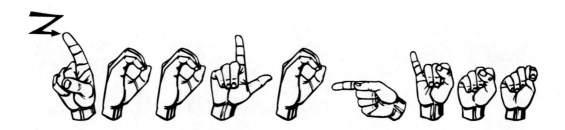

zoologist – zoólogo

Community and School

Common Classroom Signs

-

Senáles de Comunes en Clases

Bring the fingers of the dominant modified "X" handshape, palm facing reference side, with a wiggly movement from the heel to the fingers of the reference open hand held in front of the body, palm facing up. Then bring both hands, palms facing each other, downward along the sides of the body with a parallel movement.

[Sign: write + agent]

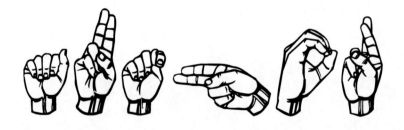

author –escritor

Community and School

Then with both "B" handshapes together in front of the chest, palms facing forward and fingers pointing up, move the hands apart in front of each shoulder.

blackboard/chalkboard - pizarra

Community and School

Starting with both palms touching in front of the chest, fingers pointing forward move the hands apart, keeping the little fingers together.

[As if opening a book]

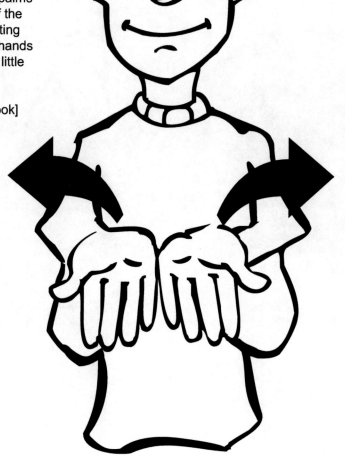

book - libro

Community and School  117

Place the fingers of the "H" handshape gently on top of the reference "H" handshape, palms facing down.

[As if two legs are dangling from a bench]

chair – silla

Move the dominant modified "X" handshape held in front of the body, palm facing forward, from the dominant to the reference side in a short up and down movement.

[As if writing on a chalkboard]

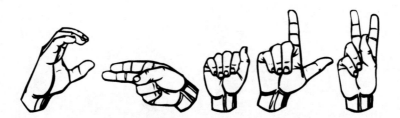

chalk - tiza

Community and School  119

Start with both "C" handshapes in front of the chest, palms facing forward and index fingers almost touching bring the hands away from each other in outwards arcs while turning the palms in, ending with the little fingers nearly touching one another. Then with both open handshapes in front of body, palms facing each other, move the hands in opposite directions by bending the wrists, ending with the reference hand near the chest and the dominant hand several inches forward of the reference hand, both palms facing in.

classroom – salón de clase

Community and School

Move the thumb side of the dominant "C" handshape, palm facing reference, from touching the lower part of the extended reference arm upward to touch the bicep.

computer - computadora

Community and School  121

Place the dominant "5" handshape in front of the mouth, palm facing in, and wiggle the fingers as the hand moves away slightly.
Then bring the fingers of the dominant modified "X" handshape, palm facing reference side, with a wiggly movement from the heel to the fingers of the reference open hand held in front of the body, palm facing up.

[Sign: colors + write]

crayon – crayola

Copyright © 2008 Time to Sign, Inc.

Community and School

Start with both "B" handshapes in front of each side of the chest, palms facing each other and fingers pointing up, bend the hands sharply ending with the reference hand above the dominant hand, both palms facing down.

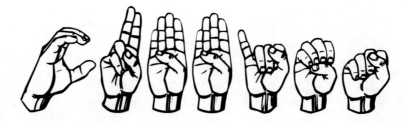

cubbies - taquillas

Community and School

Pat the forearm of the bent dominant arm with a double movement on the bent reference arm held across the chest, palms facing down. Then beginning with the fingertips of both hands touching in front of the chest, palms facing down, move the hands apart, then down, ending with palms facing each other.

[Sign: table + shape of a desk]

desk - escritorio

Move the extended dominant little finger, palm facing reference, with a wiggly movement down the palm of the reference open hand from the thumb to the little finger side.

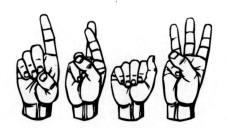

draw - dibujar

Community and School 125

Bring the knuckles of both "10" handshapes against each other, palms facing the body, in a slightly upward motion.

[As if two people facing each other in competition.]

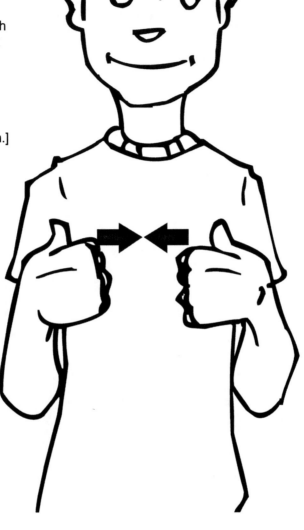

game - juego

Community and School

Move the fingertips of the dominant "G" handshape, palm and fingers facing down, over the upturned reference open hand.

[Represents spreading glue on paper]

[You can also fingerspell G-L-U-E]

glue – cola

Community and School

Tap the fingertips of the dominant bent handshape, palm facing down, on the dominant side of the forehead.

[Indicates location of knowledge in the brain]

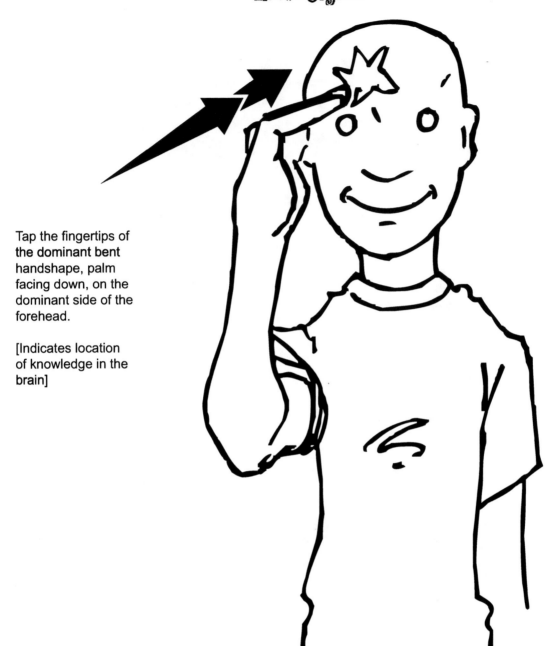

know – saber

Community and School

Start with the fingertips of the dominant curved "5" handshape, palm facing down, on the palm of the upturned reference open hand, bring the dominant hand up in the shape of a flattened "O" handshape to the forehead.

[As if taking something from a book and "putting" it in your head]

learn – aprender

Community and School

Move the pinky-finger side of the dominant bent hand, palm facing in, from the fingers to the heel of the open reference hand, palm facing up.

lesson - lección

Move the dominant open "5" handshape, palm facing in, back and forth with a double movement across the length of the bent reference forearm held in front of the body, palm facing up.

[Also: song, sing]

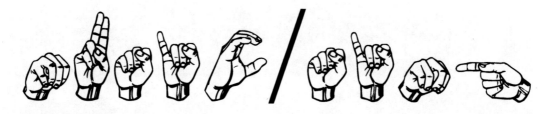

music/sing – música/cantar

Community and School  131

Touch the middle finger side of the dominant "H" handshape on top of the index finger side of the reference "H" handshape.

name - nombre

Bring the fingertips of the dominant open handshape down the length of the reference hand palm with a double movement, pulling the back of the dominant hand fingers up the reference hand palm to the fingertips each time.

[As if your dominant hand is painting the palm of your reference hand]

paint – pintura

Community and School  133

Sweep the heel of the dominant "5" handshape, palm down, back against the heel of the upturned reference "5" handshape with an upward motion.

paper - papel

Copyright © 2008 Time to Sign, Inc.

Bring the fingers of the dominant "P" handshape, palm facing reference side, with a wiggly movement from the heel to the fingers of the reference open hand held in front of the body, palm facing up.

[Initialized sign]

pen – bolígrafo

Community and School

Touch the fingertips of the dominant modified "X" handshape, palm facing in, near the mouth. Then move the dominant hand smoothly down and across the upturned reference open hand from the heel to off the fingertips.

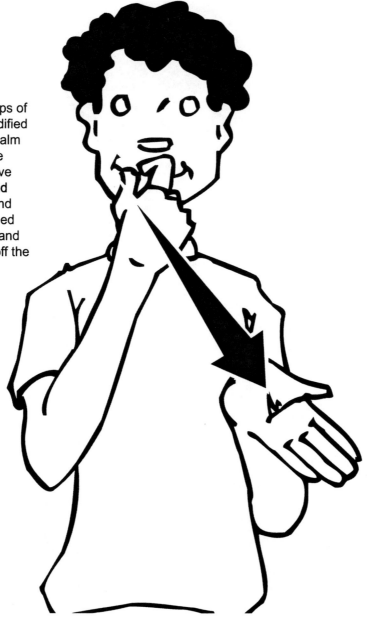

pencil – lapíz

Move both open hands from in front of the reference side of the body, palms facing each other and fingers pointing forward, in a long smooth movement to in front of the dominant side of the body.

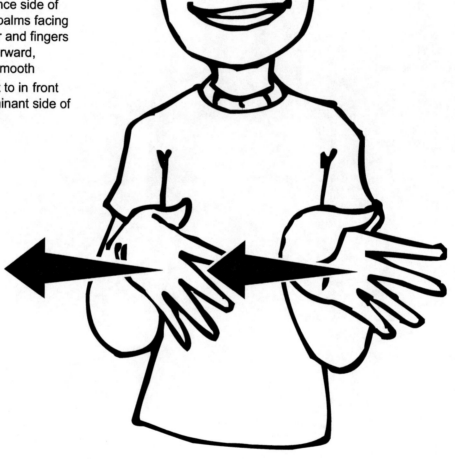

plan – planear

Community and School

Swing both "Y" handshapes up and down by twisting the wrists in front of each side of the body with a repeated movement. Then begin with the middle fingertips of both "P" handshapes touching in front of the body, palms facing each other, move the hands apart in a circular movement back until they touch again near the chest.

[Sign: play + place]

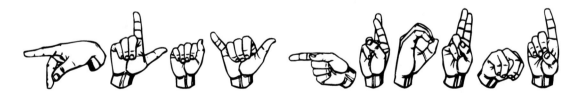

playground – patio de recreo

Start with the dominant flattened "O" handshape, palm facing forward, in front of the dominant shoulder and open and close the fingers a few times.

[As if a puppet is talking]

puppet - títere

Community and School  139

Start with the extended fingertips of both "H" handshapes touching in front of the chest, dominant palm facing forward and reference palm facing in, twist the hands in opposite directions to reverse positions with a double movement.

puzzle – rompecabezas

Copyright © 2008 Time to Sign, Inc.

Move the fingertips of the dominant "V" handshape, palm facing down, from the fingertips to the heel of the reference open hand, palm facing dominant side.

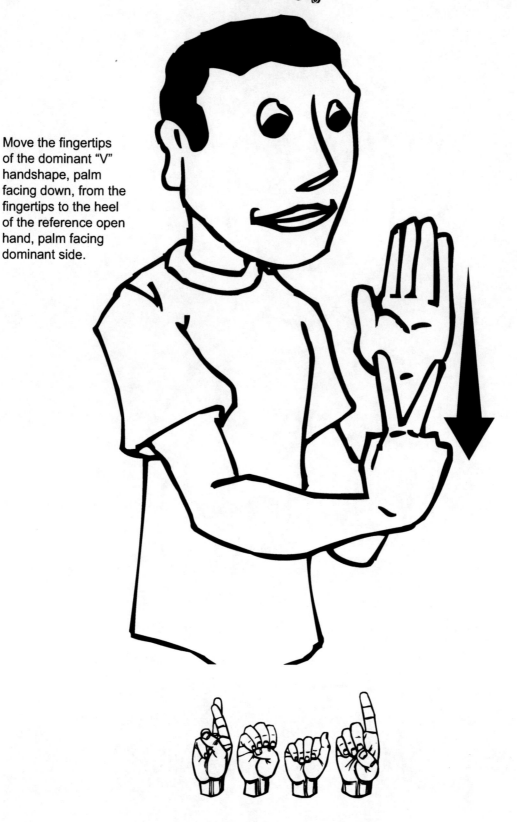

read – leer

Community and School

Begin with the reference open hand held in front of the reference shoulder, palm facing dominant side and fingers pointing forward, bring the fingers of the dominant "4" handshape, palms facing reference, down the heel of the reference hand, and then drag the back of the dominant fingers across the length of the reference palm from heel to the fingertips.

schedule – calendario

Community and School

Open and close the index and middle fingers of the dominant "V" handshape, palm facing in and fingers pointing towards reference, with a repeated movement.

[Mimic cutting with scissors]

scissors – tijeras

Copyright © 2008 Time to Sign, Inc.

Community and School

Tap the fingers of the dominant open hand, palm facing down, with a double movement of the upturned palm of the reference open hand.

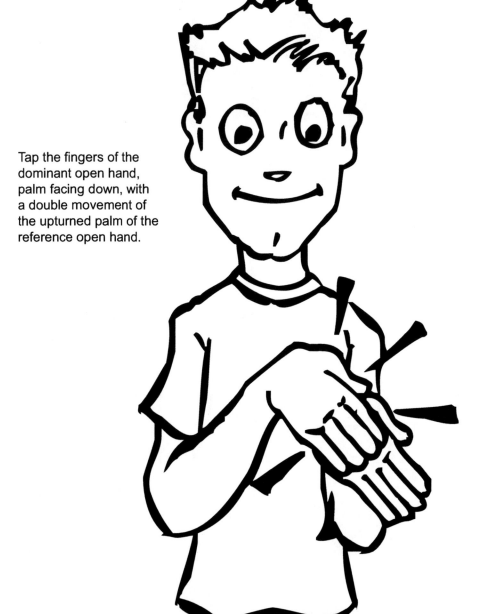

school - escuela

Start with the index-finger sides of both "B" handshapes touching in front of the chest, palms facing down and fingers pointing forward; bring the hands apart to in front of each side of the chest.

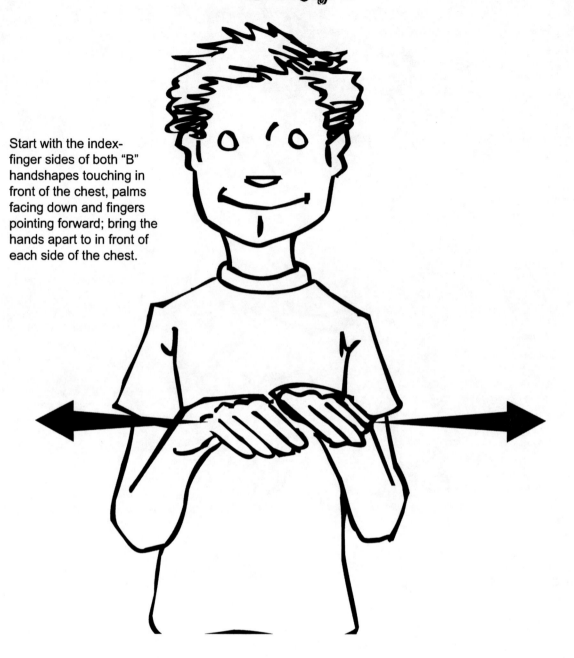

shelf – estante

Community and School 145

Begin with the fingertips of the dominant "V" handshape touching the upturned palm of the reference open hand, push the dominant fingers forward, ending with the dominant palm on the reference palm.

slide – deslizar

Community and School

Start with both flattened "C" handshapes in front of the chest, palms facing one another, and the dominant hand slightly above the reference, close the fingertips to the thumbs of each hand and then pull the hands apart in front of each shoulder with a double movement.

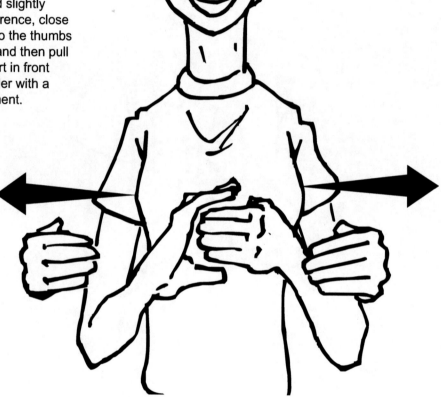

story - cuento

Community and School

Pat the forearm of the bent dominant arm with a double movement on the bent reference arm held across the chest.

table - mesa

Move both flattened "O" handshapes, palms facing each other, forward with a small double movement in front of each side of the head.

[The hands seem to take information from the head and direct it to another person]

teach - enseñar

Community and School

Move both flattened "O" handshapes, palms facing each other, forward with a small double movement in front of each side of the head. Then start with both open handshapes facing each other at shoulder height, move both hands down simultaneously.

[Sign: teach + agent]

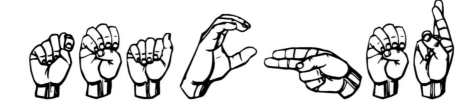

teacher – maestro(a)

Tap the extended dominant index finger to the dominant side of the forehead with a short double movement.

think – pensar

Community and School 151

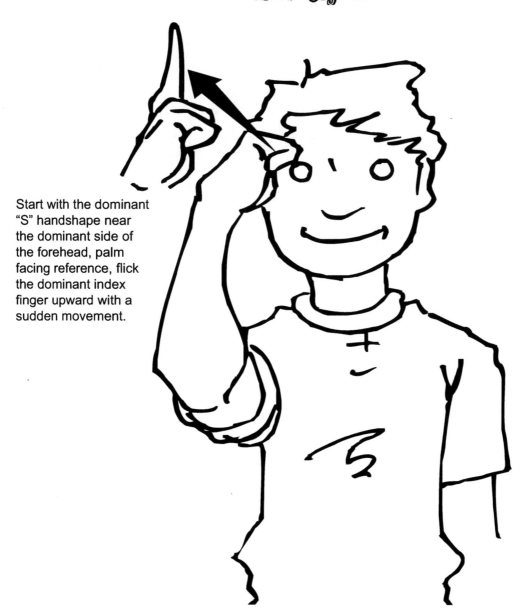

Start with the dominant "S" handshape near the dominant side of the forehead, palm facing reference, flick the dominant index finger upward with a sudden movement.

understand - entender

Touch the mouth with the index finger of the dominant "W" handshape a few times, palm facing reference. Then with the dominant hand raised slightly above the reference arm, move the dominant arm down onto the reference arm, palms facing down.

 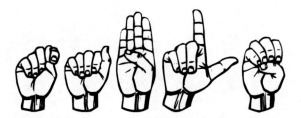

water table – mesa de agua

Community and School  153

Days of the Week Signs

-

Los Días de la Semana

Copyright © 2008 Time to Sign, Inc.

Beginning with both open hands in front of each shoulder, palms facing forward and fingers pointing up, move the hands forward in small inward circles.

[The movement of the hands shows reverence and awe]

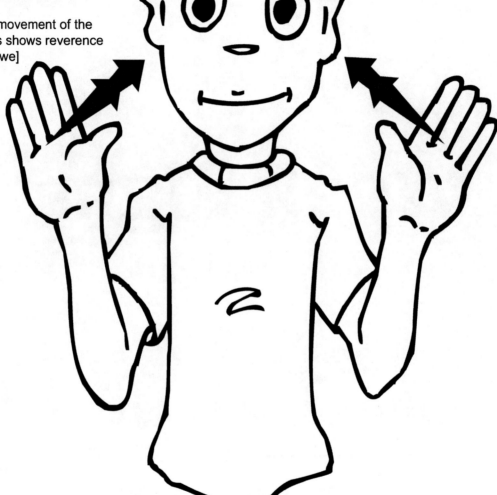

Sunday - Domingo

Community and School

Move the dominant "M" hand, palm facing in, in a double circle in front of the dominant shoulder.

[Initialize sign]

Monday - Lunes

156   **Community and School**

Move the dominant "T" hand, palm facing in, in a circle in front of the dominant shoulder.

[Initialize sign]

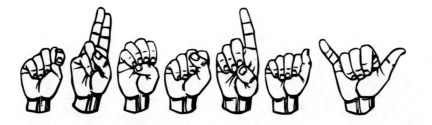

Tuesday - Martes

Community and School

Move the dominant "W" hand, palm facing in and fingers pointing up, in a circle in front of the dominant shoulder.

[Initialize sign]

Wednesday - Miércoles

Copyright © 2008 Time to Sign, Inc.

Beginning with the dominant "T" hand in front of the dominant shoulder, palm facing forward and in a small circle, quickly switch to the "H" hand and continue the circle, palm facing in.

[Abbreviation "T" + "H"]

Thursday - Jueves

Community and School

Move the dominant "F" hand, palm facing in, in a repeated circle in front of the dominant shoulder.

[Initialize sign]

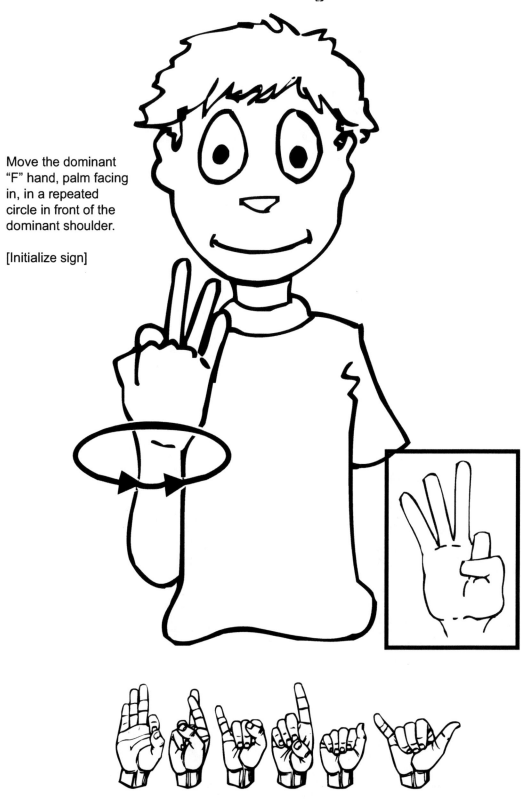

Friday - Viernes

Community and School

Move the dominant "S" hand, palm facing out, in a small circle in front of the dominant shoulder.

[Initialize sign]

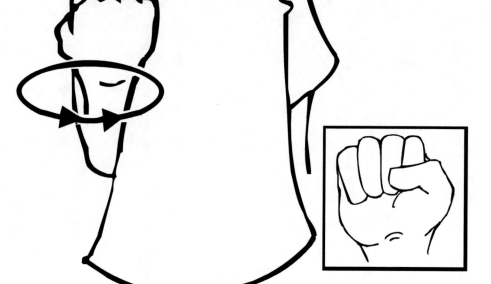

Saturday - Sábado

Community and School  161

Functional & Directional Signs

-

Funcional y Direciónal Señales

Move the **dominant open hand**, palm angled in, towards the dominant shoulder.

[Come on, natural gesture motioning someone to come]

come – venir

Community and School  163

Point down with the dominant index finger.

down – abajo

Community and School

Begin with both extended index fingers held in front of the body, fingers pointing up and palms facing each other, reference in front of the dominant hand, move the hands forward in a small arc.

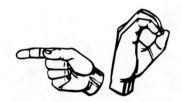

go – ir

Community and School 165

Point the dominant index finger towards the ear.

[As if showing the ear to listen]

[Also: ear]

hear – oír

The dominant open "5" handshape, facing the body and pointing down becomes a flat "O" handshape, as it moves in through the reference "C" handshape which then becomes an "O" handshape.

inside - adentro

Community and School  167

Beginning with the bent dominant hand, palm and fingers facing inward, closer to the chest than the same positioned reference hand, move the dominant hand up and over the reference hand.

[Mimics overcoming an obstacle to move along to the next thing]

next – luego, después

Copyright © 2008 Time to Sign, Inc.

Community and School

Bring the dominant index finger, middle finger and thumb together in one motion, palm facing forward.

no - no

Community and School

Begin with the dominant "5" handshape, palm facing down, inserted in the reference "C" handshape, palm facing reference, bring the dominant hand upward, closing the fingers and thumb into a flattened "O" handshape.

outside – afuera

Community and School

Starting with the dominant curved "5" handshape inserted in the palm side of reference curved "5" handshape, palm facing towards the dominant side of the body, bring the dominant hand upward while closing the thumb and index finger, forming an "F" handshape.

pick/find - encontrar

Community and School

Start with the flattened "O" handshapes in front of the body, palms facing down, move both hands upward and forward in a small arc.

put - poner

Hook the index finger of the dominant "L" handshape under the thumb of the reference "L" handshape and move both hands forward in a quick short motion.

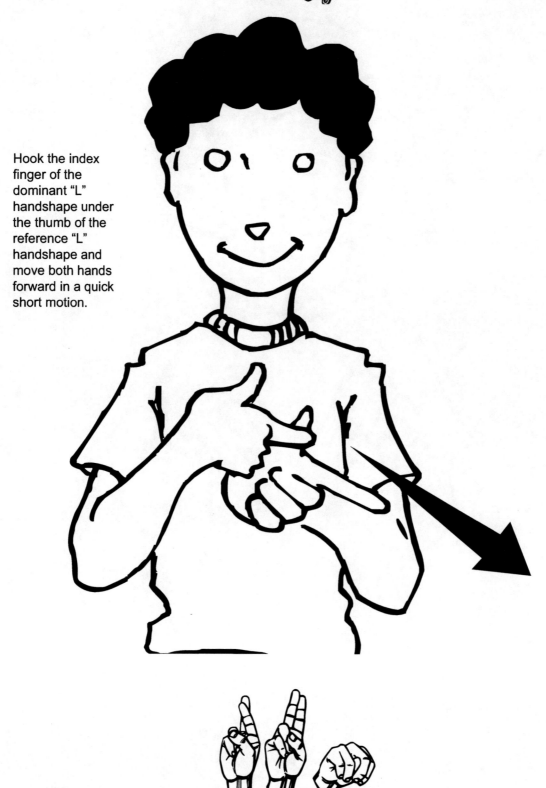

run – correr

Community and School  173

With dominant '1' handshape, touch the chin with the index finger and hold it in place.

[Also: speak, say]

said/say – dicho, decir

Copyright © 2008 Time to Sign, Inc.

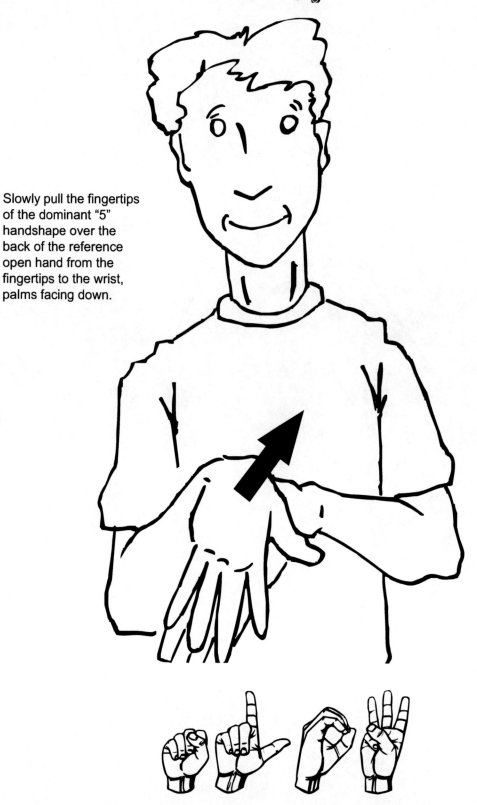

Slowly pull the fingertips of the dominant "5" handshape over the back of the reference open hand from the fingertips to the wrist, palms facing down.

slow - lento

Community and School

Point up with the index finger of the dominant hand.

up – hacia arriba, arriba

Begin with both "5" handshapes in front of the body, palms facing up and fingers pointing forward, bring the hands back toward the chest while constricting the fingers toward the palms.

[As if gesturing to bring something to you]

want –querer

Community and School  177

Shake the dominant "S" handshape from the wrist up and down in front of the dominant shoulder, palm facing forward.

[As if nodding your hand]

yes - sí

Copyright © 2008 Time to Sign, Inc.

Months Signs - Señales de los Meses

Community and School  179

The dominant "J" handshape, palm facing in, arcs over the vertically held reference open hand, palm facing in.

January - Enero

Copyright © 2008 Time to Sign, Inc.

The dominant "F" handshape, palm facing forward, arcs over the vertically held reference open hand, palm facing in.

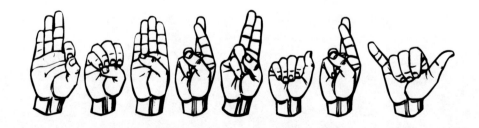

February - Febrero

Community and School  181

The dominant "M" handshape, palm facing forward, arcs over the vertically held reference open hand, palm facing in.

March - Marzo

Copyright © 2008 Time to Sign, Inc.

The dominant "A" handshape, palm facing forward, arcs over the vertically held reference open hand,

palm facing in.

April - Abril

Community and School  183

The dominant "M" handshape arcs to a "Y" handshape, palm facing forward, as the dominant hand arcs over the vertically held reference open hand, palm facing in.

May - Mayo

Copyright © 2008 Time to Sign, Inc.

Community and School

The dominant "J" handshape arcs to an "N" handshape, as the dominant hand arcs over the vertically held reference open hand, palm facing in.

June - Junio

Community and School  185

The dominant "J" handshape arcs to a "Y" handshape as the dominant hand arcs over the vertically held reference open hand, palm facing in.

July - Julio

Copyright © 2008 Time to Sign, Inc.

The dominant "A" handshape arcs to a "G" handshape, palm facing forward, as the dominant hand arcs over the vertically held reference open hand, palm facing in.

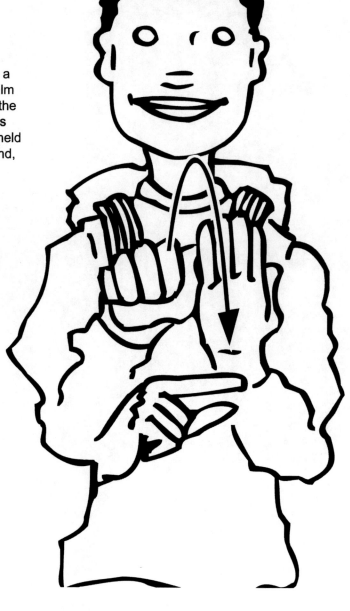

August – Agosto

Community and School  187

The dominant "S" handshape, palm facing forward, arcs over the vertically held reference open hand, palm facing in.

September - Septiembre

Copyright © 2008 Time to Sign, Inc.

The dominant "O" handshape, palm facing reference, arcs over the vertically held reference open hand, palm facing in.

October - Octubre

Community and School

189

The dominant "N" handshape, palm facing forward, arcs over the vertically held reference open hand, palm facing in.

November - Noviembre

Copyright © 2008 Time to Sign, Inc.

The dominant "D" handshape, palm facing forward, arcs over the vertically held reference open hand, palm facing in.

December - Diciembre

Community and School

Time & Day Signs

-

Señales De Distintos Horarios del Día

With the bottom of the dominant forearm resting on the back of the reference open hand, palm facing down, move the dominant open hand downward with a double movement.

afternoon - tarde

Community and School 193

Starting with the bent dominant elbow resting on the back of the reference hand across the body, palm facing down; bring the extended dominant index-finger from pointing up in front of the dominant shoulder, palm facing reference, downward towards the reference elbow.

day – día

Slide forward the bent middle finger of the dominant "5" handshape, palm facing down, across the back of the open reference hand, palm facing down.

[Mimics a bird hopping around looking for food – the early bird]

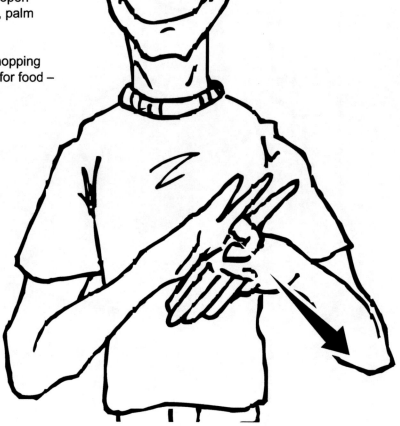

early – temprano

Community and School  195

Tap the heel of the dominant bent hand, palm facing forward, with a double movement against the thumb side of the reference open hand held across the chest, palm facing down.

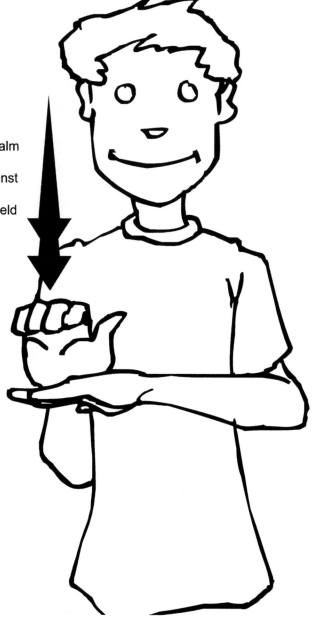

evening – atardecer

Copyright © 2008 Time to Sign, Inc.

Move the palm side of the dominant "A" handshape forward on the dominant side of the chin with a repeated movement.

everyday – todos los días

Community and School  197

With the dominant index-finger extended, palm facing in, move the palm side of the dominant hand in a circle on the palm of the open reference hand, palm facing in, while twisting the wrist, ending with the dominant palm facing in again.

[Represents index finger moving on a clock]

hour – hora

Copyright © 2008 Time to Sign, Inc.

198  **Community and School**

With the thumb of the dominant "L" handshape, palm facing forward, on the palm of the reference open hand, palm facing reference and fingers pointing forward, twist the dominant hand forward, keeping the thumb in place and ending with the dominant palm facing down.

later – más

Copyright © 2008 Time to Sign, Inc.

Community and School

Move the extended dominant index finger, palm facing reference, forward a short distance, pivoting the closed fingers of the dominant hand on the palm of the reference open hand, palm facing reference and fingers pointing up.

minute – minuto

Move the extended dominant index finger, palm facing in and fingers pointing to the reference side, from the tip to the base of the extended reference finger, palm facing dominant side and fingers pointing up in front of the chest.

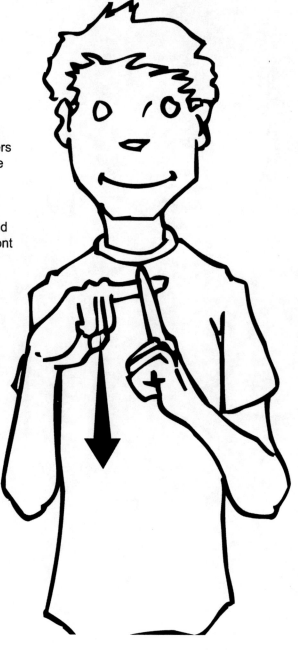

month – mes

Community and School

Bring the dominant "5" handshape from the mouth down to the upward turned palm of the reference palm in front of the chest. Then with the reference open hand in the crook of the bent dominant arm, bring the dominant open handshapes upward, palm facing in.

morning – mañana

Tap the heel of the dominant hand with a double movement on the index-finger side of the back of the reference hand, palms facing down.

[Also: tonight]

night – noche

Community and School  203

Start with "Y" handshapes out from the body, palms facing up, move both hands downward to the sides of the body.

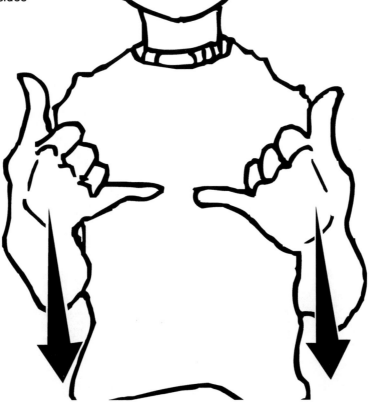

now – ahora

Copyright © 2008 Time to Sign, Inc.

Community and School

With the palm side of the dominant "1" handshape against the reference open palm, fingers pointing up, twist the extended dominant finger forward a very short distance.

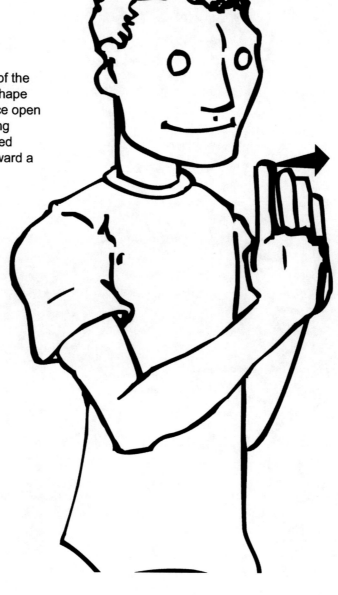

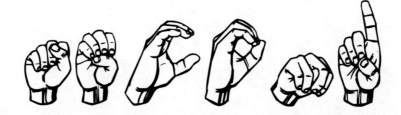

second – segundo

Community and School

Tap the index finger of the dominant "X" handshape on the wrist of the reference hand, palms facing down, with a double movement.

time – tiempo

Start with both "Y" handshapes, palms facing up, bring both hands down with a short double movement in front of each side of the body.
[Sign: now + day]

today – hoy

Community and School

Move the palm side of the dominant "10" handshape, palm facing in, from the dominant side of the chin forward while twisting the wrist forward.

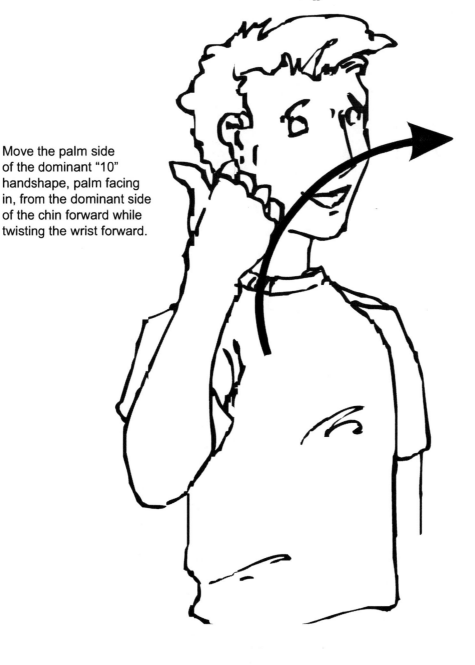

tomorrow – mañana

Copyright © 2008 Time to Sign, Inc.

Community and School

Slide the palm side of the dominant "1" hand, palm facing down, from thumb across the fingers of the reference open hand, palm facing up.

week – semana

Community and School

Begin with the dominant "S" handshape, over the reference "S" handshape, palms facing opposite directions, move the dominant hand forward in a complete circle around the reference hand while the reference hand moves in a small circle around the dominant hand, ending with the dominant hand back on top of the reference hand.

year – año

Touch the dominant side of the cheek with the thumb of the dominant "Y" handshape, palm facing forward, from the dominant side of the chin to the dominant cheek.

[The "A" hand can be used for this sign as well]

yesterday – ayer

Community and School  **211**

Common Classroom Phrases

Common Classroom Phrases

Community and School  213

Common Classroom Phrases

Common Classroom Phrases

Common Classroom Phrases

Common Classroom Phrases

Community and School  217

Common Classroom Phrases

Common Classroom Phrases

Common Classroom Phrases

Community and School  221

Common Classroom Phrases

Common Classroom Phrases

Community and School

Common Classroom Phrases

Common Classroom Phrases

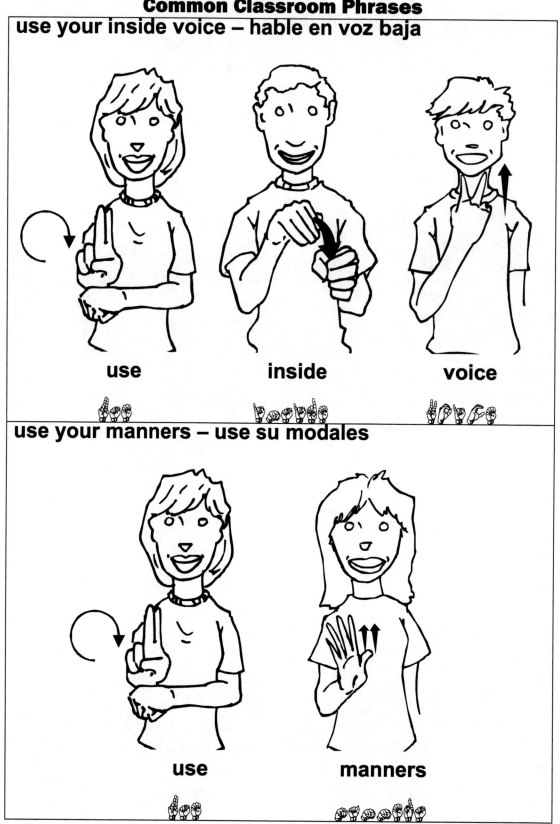

Community and School  225

Common Classroom Phrases

SIGN LANGUAGE HANDOUT
CONSTRUCTION

build - construir

dirt – tierra

move – mudarse

tools – herramientas

truck - camión

Community and School  227

SIGN LANGUAGE HANDOUT
HEALTH CARE

dentist – dentista

doctor - doctor

earache - dolor de oídos

hospital - hospital

hurt – herido

nurse – enfermera

sick – enfermo

Copyright © 2008 Time to Sign, Inc.

SIGN LANGUAGE HANDOUT
MAIL/POST OFFICE

letter – carta

mailbox – buzón

mail carrier – cartero

post office – oficina de correos

stamp – estampilla

write – escribir

Copyright © 2008 Time to Sign, Inc.

Community and School  **229**

SIGN LANGUAGE HANDOUT
PLACES

bank – banco

church - iglesia

library – biblioteca

restaurant - restaurante

store – tienda

Copyright © 2008 Time to Sign, Inc.

SIGN LANGUAGE HANDOUT
COMMUNITY PEOPLE

firefighter - bombero

friend – amigo

neighbor - vecino

librarian - bibliotecario

police - policía

Copyright © 2008 Time to Sign, Inc.

Community and School  231

SIGN LANGUAGE HANDOUT
OCCUPATIONS

accountant - contador

actor - actor

architect - arquitecto

artist - artista

astronaut - astronauta

Copyright © 2008 Time to Sign, Inc.

SIGN LANGUAGE HANDOUT
OCCUPATIONS

baker - panaderío

barber - barbero

banker - banquero

captain - capitán

caregiver - cuidador

Copyright © 2008 Time to Sign, Inc.

Community and School 233

SIGN LANGUAGE HANDOUT
OCCUPATIONS

carpenter - carpintero

computer person – programador

cashier - cajero

crossing guard – guardia de transito escolar

Copyright © 2008 Time to Sign, Inc.

SIGN LANGUAGE HANDOUT
OCCUPATIONS

engineer - ingeniero

florist - florista

forester - guarda bosques

historian - historiador

Community and School  **235**

SIGN LANGUAGE HANDOUT
OCCUPATIONS

interpreter - intéprete

journalist - periodista

judge - juez

lawyer - abogado

Copyright © 2008 Time to Sign, Inc.

SIGN LANGUAGE HANDOUT
OCCUPATIONS

painter - pintor

park ranger – policia de parques

pastor – pastor

p.e. teacher – maestro de educación física

Community and School  237

SIGN LANGUAGE HANDOUT
OCCUPATIONS

photographer - fotógrafo

pilot - piloto

politician - político

president - presidente

principal - principal

Copyright © 2008 Time to Sign, Inc.

SIGN LANGUAGE HANDOUT
OCCUPATIONS

reporter - reportero

scientist - científico

secretary - secretario(a)

sing/musician – cantante, músico

Community and School  239

SIGN LANGUAGE HANDOUT
OCCUPATIONS

student – estudiante

veterinarian – veterinario

volunteer - voluntario

zoologist - zoólogo

Copyright © 2008 Time to Sign, Inc.

SIGN LANGUAGE HANDOUT
LEARNING

learn - aprender

lesson - lección

teach - enseñar

think - pensar

Community and School  241

SIGN LANGUAGE HANDOUT
CLASSROOM

classroom - salon de clase

cubbies - taquillas

blackboard/chalkboard - pizarra

chair - silla

table - mesa

Copyright © 2008 Time to Sign, Inc.

SIGN LANGUAGE HANDOUT
SCHOOL BEHAVIOR

quiet - silencio

sit - sentarse

share - compartir

stop - parar

SIGN LANGUAGE HANDOUT
SCHOOL

boy - niño

girl - niña

friend - amigo

school - escuela

teacher - maestro(a)

SIGN LANGUAGE HANDOUT
SCHOOL ACTIVITIES

game - juego

music - música

puzzle - rompecabezas

toys - juguete

Copyright © 2008 Time to Sign, Inc.

Community and School　

SIGN LANGUAGE HANDOUT
READING

book - libro

story - cuento

read - leer

Copyright © 2008 Time to Sign, Inc.

SIGN LANGUAGE HANDOUT
ART SIGNS

chalk - tiza

crayon - crayola

draw - dibujar

paint - pintura

paper - papel

scissors - tijeras

Copyright © 2008 Time to Sign, Inc.

Community and School  247

SIGN LANGUAGE HANDOUT
SCHOOL BEHAVIOR

come here please
- ven aqui por favor

don't throw - no tire

don't push - no empujes

wait please – espera por favor

Copyright © 2008 Time to Sign, Inc.

SIGN LANGUAGE HANDOUT
SCHOOL BEHAVIOR

don't touch – no toque

good work - buen trabajo

terrific - magnifico

I am proud of you
- estoy orgulloso(a) de ti

SIGN LANGUAGE HANDOUT
SCHOOL BEHAVIOR

more please - más por favor

thank you - gracias

use your manners - use sus modales

SIGN LANGUAGE HANDOUT
SCHOOL BEHAVIOR

careful please - tengan cuidado

**say you are sorry
- digale que lo siente**

I'm sorry - perdóname

Community and School  251

SIGN LANGUAGE HANDOUT
SCHOOL BEHAVIOR

snack time - tiempo de merendar

time to eat - tiempo de comer

time to go - vamonos

Copyright © 2008 Time to Sign, Inc.

SIGN LANGUAGE HANDOUT
SCHOOL BEHAVIOR

time to sign - tiempo de usar señales

playtime - tiempo de jugar

Community and School  253

SIGN LANGUAGE HANDOUT
DAYS

| Sunday - Domingo | Monday - Lunes | Tuesday - Martes |

| Wednesday - Miércoles | Thursday - Jueves | Friday - Viernes | Saturday - Sábado |

Seven Days in a Week
Traditional Song, tune of Clementine

There are seven days, there are seven days,
there are seven days in a week.
Sunday, Monday, Tuesday, Wednesday,
Thursday, Friday, Saturday.

Copyright © 2008 Time to Sign, Inc.

SIGN LANGUAGE
HANDOUT - MONTHS

January - Enero

February - Febrero

March - Marzo

April - Abril

May - Mayo

June - Junio

Copyright © 2008 Time to Sign, Inc.

Community and School  255

SIGN LANGUAGE
HANDOUT - MONTHS

July - Julio

August - Agosto

September - Septiembre

October - Octubre

November - Noviembre

December - Deciembre

Copyright © 2008 Time to Sign, Inc.

SIGN LANGUAGE HANDOUT – TIME

day - día

hour - hora

minute - minuto

time - tiempo

week - semana

Community and School  257

SIGN LANGUAGE
HANDOUT – DAYS

today - hoy

tomorrow - mañana

yesterday - ayer

Copyright © 2008 Time to Sign, Inc.

Index

Symbols

911 55

A

accountant 74, 231
actor 75, 231
address 47
afternoon 192
ambulance 38
April 182, 254
architect 76, 231
artist 77, 231
astronaut 78, 231
August 186, 255
author 114

B

badge 39
baker 79, 232
bank 29, 229
banker 80, 232
barber 81, 232
better 56
blackboard 115, 241
body 57
book 116, 245
boy 243
build 68, 226

C

captain 82, 232
careful please 217, 250
caregiver 83, 232
carpenter 84, 233
cashier 85, 233
chair 117, 241
chalk 118, 246
chalkboard 115, 241
church 30, 229
classroom 119, 241
clean up time 211
come 162
come here please 247
come here please/now 212
computer 120
computer person 86, 233
crayon 121, 246
crossing guard 87, 233
cubbies 122, 241

D

day 193, 256
December 190, 255
dentist 58, 227
desk 123
dirt 69, 226
doctor 59, 227
don't push 247
don't throw 247
don't throw/push 212
don't touch 217, 248
down 163
draw 124, 246

E

earache 227
early 194
engineer 88, 234
evening 195
everyday 196

F

February 180, 254
feel 60
find 170
fire 40
fire engine 42
firefighter 41, 230
florist 89, 234
forester 90, 234
Friday 159, 253
friend 31, 230, 243

G

game 125, 244
girl 243
glue 126
go 164
good work 214, 248

H

head 61
hear 165
help 43
historian 91, 234
hospital 62, 227
hour 197, 256
hurt 63, 227

I

I am proud of you 214, 248
I'm sorry 220, 250
inside 166
interpreter 92, 235

J

January 179, 254
journalist 93, 235
judge 94, 235
July 185, 255
June 184, 254

K

know 127

L

later 198
lawyer 95, 235
learn 128, 240
lesson 129, 240
letter 48, 228
librarian 96, 230
library 32, 229
line up please 215

M

mail 48
mailbox 49, 228
mail carrier 50, 228
March 181, 254
May 183, 254
minute 199, 256
Monday 155, 253
month 200
more please 215, 249
morning 201
move 70, 226
music 130, 244
musician 109, 238

N

name 131
nap-time 216
neighbor 33, 230
next 167
night 202

Copyright © 2008 Time to Sign, Inc.

Community and School

Index

no 168
November 189, 255
now 203
nurse 64, 227

O

October 188, 255
outside 169

P

paint 132, 246
painter 97, 236
paper 133, 246
park 34
park ranger 98, 236
pastor 99, 236
pay attention please 216
pen 134
pencil 135
p.e. teacher 100, 236
photographer 101, 237
pick 170
pilot 102, 237
plan 136
playground 137
play time 219
playtime 252
police 44, 230
politician 103, 237
post office 51, 228
president 104, 237
principal 105, 237
puppet 138
put 171
puzzle 139, 244

Q

quiet 242
quiet please 219

R

read 140, 245
reporter 106, 238
restaurant 35, 229
run 172

S

safety 45
said 173
Saturday 160, 253
say 173
say you are sorry 220, 250
schedule 141
school 143, 243
scientist 107, 238
scissors 142, 246
second 204
secretary 108, 238
September 187, 255
share 242
share please 220
shelf 144
sick 65, 227
sing 130, 238
singer 109
sit 242
sit in a circle 19, 211
sit still 218
slide 145
slow 174
snack time 221, 251
stamp 52, 228
stop 242
stop now 221
store 36, 229
story 146, 245
story time 222
student 239
Sunday 154, 253

T

table 147, 241
teach 148, 240
teacher 149, 243
teeth 66
terrific 248
thank you 249
think 150, 240
Thursday 158, 253
time 205, 256
time to eat 222, 251
time to go 223, 251
time to go inside 213
time to go outside 213
time to sign 223, 252
today 206, 257

tomorrow 207, 257
tools 71, 226
toys 244
truck 72, 226
Tuesday 156, 253

U

understand 151
up 175
use your inside voice 224
use your manners 224, 249
use your words 225

V

veterinarian 110, 239
volunteer 111, 239

W

wait 218
wait please 247
walk please 225
want 176
water table 152
Wednesday 157, 253
week 208, 256
write 53, 228

Y

year 209
yes 177
yesterday 210, 257

Z

zoologist 112, 239

Copyright © 2008 Time to Sign, Inc.

Our Original Learning Books

Time to Sign with Children Learning Guide

The Learning Guide is a great beginner book for teachers and parents. It covers how to incorporate Sign Language into your daily routine and includes developmental communication milestones and age-appropriate signs and activities from birth to five years. Features over 200 sign illustrations, including the alphabet, animals, emotions, family signs, manners, food, and much more. The book also comes with a DVD to demonstrate all signs in the book!

The original Time to Sign Learning Books Series covers all ages of children, from infant to school-age, and all feature English, Spanish, and Sign.

Time to Sign Preschool Sign Language Book

This book has over 300 sign illustrations that are specific to the preschool learning environment. Children learn how to use American Sign Language (ASL) to communicate: manners, emotions, family, colors, transportation, opposites, and much more. Teachers learn signs for classroom management.

Time to Sign School Age Sign Language Book

This book contains nearly 1000 sign illustrations for school age children. With age-appropriate signs to include such areas as: Occupations, insects, pronouns, questions, seasons, sports, math, science, common signs and phrases, and much more.

Time to Sign, Inc.
PO Box 33831
Indialantic, FL 32903
Phone 321.259.0976
www.timetosign.com

Contact us at 321.259.0976 or contact@timetosign.com for more information!

Signing Walk with DVD

A Journey into Nature through Sign Language

On this fun and educational DVD, follow J.K. on his walk in the woods. Learn signs for various animals, insects, colors, and more! Also includes songs such as Twinkle, Twinle Little Star and Itsy Bitsy Spider. Book provides pictures and descriptions of all the signs shown in the DVD as well as the signs for the songs.

Take a walk through nature and learn sign language as you go!

Time to Sign

PO Box 33831
Indialantic, FL 32903
Phone 321.259.0976
www.timetosign.com

Contact us at 321.259.0976 or contact@timetosign.com for more information!

Christian Signs Book with CD & DVD

Learn signs for any Christian-based program!

This book contains over 100 large illustrated signs and 14 songs with an accompanying music CD and DVD that demonstrates all songs and signs in the book! Great for use at home or in church, Sunday School, or any Christian-based program! The Christian Signing Book features large 8.5" x 11" pictures for all signs, as well as both English and Spanish.

Add this fun and meaningful book to your family collection, Sunday School class, or choir for worship service.

Songs Include: All Things Bright & Beautiful; The B-I-B-L-E; Bless That Wonderful Name; Deep & Wide; I've Got the Joy; God is So Good; I Love You; Jesus Loves the Little Children; Oh, How I Love Jesus; Peace Like a River; Praise Him in the Morning; Praise Him, Praise Him; All Ye Little Children; Rejoice in the Lord Always; This is My Father's World.

Time to Sign inc.™

PO Box 33831
Indialantic, FL 32903
Phone 321.259.0976
www.timetosign.com

Contact us at 321.259.0976 or contact@timetosign.com for more information!

Classroom Materials

Our classroom materials help teach students and encourage further learning.

Time to Sign Pledge of Allegiance Poster
This 18" x 24" poster teaches children the nation's pledge in easy to-follow signs

Time to Sign Alphabet Wall Chart
Post this ASL alphabet on your wall to support children's learning. Features upper and lower case letters, the handshape for each letter, and a description of how to sign an example word.

Time to Sign Placemats
This set of 4 double-sided placemats feature the alphabet, animals, colors, family, numbers, school, and seasons signs. Placemats are treated with durable 5 mil thick, easy-to-clean plastic for use in eating and arts areas, or for posting on walls or glass. Over 120 signs in all!

Time to Sign Infants Small Placemat
This placemat features 18 common infant signs, such as mother, father, yes, no, please, thank you, bath, love, and milk. Placemats are treated with durable 5 mil thick, easy-to-clean plastic for use in eating and arts areas, or for posting on walls or glass.

Time to Sign

PO Box 33831
Indialantic, FL 32903
Phone 321.259.0976
www.timetosign.com

Contact us at 321.259.0976 or contact@timetosign.com for more information!